# THE DATA HANDBOOK

## A GUIDE TO UNDERSTANDING THE ORGANIZATION AND VISUALIZATION OF TECHNICAL DATA

SPYGLASS

This book was produced in Microsoft Word 5.0. We made extensive use of Spyglass Transform, Spyglass Dicer, Spyglass Format, Systat, Canvas, and Igor for the illustrations. Since Word does not support high resolution PICT graphics, we first created most illustrations at 400% size, scaled them down to 100% in Canvas, saved them as EPSF files, and then placed the EPSF files into Word.

The main text is set in 10 point Palatino, headlines are in Helvetica Narrow, and example data is in Courier. The small bird illustration was scanned in as a TIFF file, converted to EPSF in Adobe Photoshop, and then placed in the Word document. All other drawings were stripped in traditionally. The Word files were output directly to film on a phototypesetter.

# THE DATA HANDBOOK

## A GUIDE TO UNDERSTANDING THE ORGANIZATION AND VISUALIZATION OF TECHNICAL DATA

VERSION 1.0

Brand Fortner

*Illustrations by Eric Pervukhin*

Spyglass, Inc.  P.O. Box 6388, Champaign, IL 61826

# PREFACE

We all go to school and learn about our particular disciplines, be they astrophysics, geology, microbiology, chemistry, or whatever. What our teachers don't tell us in school is that we will spend most of our scientific or engineering career in front of computers, trying to beat them into submission. My formal training in computational science is *nil*, which I suspect is true of 95% of the scientists and engineers in the world.

In this book I attempt to bring together in one place the basic facts that every technical person should know about computers. The computers of today are still relatively 'dumb,' in that you must know quite a bit about them to use them effectively for technical data analysis.

Scientists and engineers who are computer novices should read this book cover to cover (that is, in my modest opinion). Experienced computer users should use this book as a reference. I guarantee that there are nuggets of useful information in this book waiting to be discovered by even the most computer literate of you.

## The Parts of the Data Handbook

Part I introduces five hypothetical researchers and their data. Their problems are used throughout the book as examples of the pitfalls and confusions of digital data storage and analysis.

Part II goes into great detail about how computers store numbers. It focuses on common problems associated with storing numbers in computers. Perhaps the most common confusion is the difference between *binary* numbers and *text* numbers.

Part III elaborates on the concept of *data dimensionality*. People that do not fully understand this concept may be missing out on much better ways of visualizing or analysing their data.

Part IV is a reference on the prevalent standard technical data formats.

Part V returns to the five researchers and ties everything together by summarizing their problems and the solutions.

## Acknowledgements

This book would not have been possible without the support of
Spyglass Inc. Jodi Asbell-Clarke did the research for Chapter 12,
Wolf Sonnenberg supplied material for Chapter 11, Tim Krauskopf
wrote most of Chapter 13, Barry Sanders did the cover design,
Kathy Robinson managed to take the raw material and shape it
into a real book, and Mike Knezovich coordinated everything.
Mark Thomas was also a great help in copyediting the material.

I would also like to acknowledge the following Spyglass people for
their assistance: Doug Colbeth, Mike Tyrrell, Maureen Blake,
Jeanne Balbach, Scott Piette, Eric Sink, Susan Tharp, Roberta
Hewerdine, Sue Sherman, Barbra King, and Cindy Garland.

Thanks to Professor Louis Wicker and Dr. David Clarke for
providing data for some of the examples in the book.

Thanks to Monica Fortner for her extensive editing and helpful
suggestions. And, of course, a special thanks to Eric Pervukhin, who
made the puffin drawings that begin each chapter.

## Send me your Comments!

Please note that this is Version 1.0 of The Data Handbook. There
will be an enhanced version of the book coming out soon, so I look
forward to your comments and suggestions! Please send them to me
at the address listed below.

*Brand Fortner*
*Champaign, IL*
*August 1992*

Brand Fortner
Spyglass, Inc.
P.O Box 6388
Champaign, IL 61826

Ph: 217/ 355-1665
FAX: 217/355-8925
Applelink: D5717
Internet:D5717@applelink.apple.com

# BRIEF CONTENTS

# CONTENTS

## PART I—INTRODUCTION

## PART II—NUMBERS IN COMPUTERS

## Chapter 4. (Cont.)

# PART III—THE DATA UNIVERSE

## Chapter 6. A Map of the Data Universe .............................. 79

# PART IV—DATA FORMATS

# PART I
## INTRODUCTION

In this Part we introduce five researchers, their projects, and their data. We will use these five projects throughout the book to illustrate the fine points of technical data analysis and organization. We pose five questions here about their numbers and their data—the same questions you are likely to have about your data. We hope this book answers those questions.

In Part V we will summarize the answers to the posed questions for these five researchers.

# PART I
# INTRODUCTION

# Five Researchers and Their Data

## Judy ReSyrch—Fan Simulation

Judy ReSyrch at the University of Dutch Harbor spent all night
running her simulations of air flow through a desk fan, as part of a
project to optimize the design of the fan and the enclosure. She
designed the simulation carefully, and now her workstation has
millions of numbers representing velocity, air pressure, blade
position, etc. But that's just the beginning. How should she store
these numbers? How should she analyze and visualize them?

**Figure I.1**
*Velocity Matrix Data*

| | 22860 | 22980 | 23100 | 23220 | 23340 | 23460 | 23580 | • • • |
|---|---|---|---|---|---|---|---|---|
| 44940 | −4.84 | −4.64 | −4.44 | −4.24 | −4.04 | −2.81 | −2.44 | • • • |
| 44820 | −4.91 | −5.44 | −5.33 | −4.64 | −4.02 | −3.12 | −2.66 | • • • |
| 44700 | −4.99 | −5.57 | −5.89 | −5.18 | −4.42 | −3.59 | −3.04 | • • • |
| 44580 | −5.07 | −5.26 | −6.11 | −5.71 | −5.06 | −4.25 | −3.58 | • • • |
| 44460 | −5.15 | −4.91 | −6.00 | −6.03 | −5.72 | −5.01 | −4.27 | • • • |
| 44340 | −5.35 | −4.73 | −5.63 | −6.03 | −6.20 | −5.76 | −5.07 | • • • |
| 44220 | −5.34 | −4.83 | −5.19 | −5.69 | −6.24 | −6.26 | −5.83 | • • • |
| 44100 | −5.33 | −5.05 | −4.93 | −5.23 | −5.84 | −6.26 | −6.26 | • • • |
| 43980 | −5.33 | −5.30 | −4.94 | −4.92 | −5.30 | −5.78 | −6.14 | • • • |
| 43860 | −5.32 | −5.45 | −5.09 | −4.86 | −4.95 | −5.21 | −5.62 | • • • |
| 43740 | −5.78 | −5.17 | −5.31 | −4.94 | −4.88 | −4.86 | −5.10 | • • • |
| 43620 | −5.35 | −4.93 | −5.34 | −5.04 | −4.96 | −4.78 | −4.79 | • • • |
| 43500 | −4.93 | −4.30 | −5.19 | −5.01 | −5.05 | −4.83 | −4.69 | • • • |
| 43380 | −4.50 | −3.55 | −4.88 | −4.78 | −5.03 | −4.91 | −4.73 | • • • |
| 43260 | −4.07 | −2.71 | −4.50 | −4.34 | −4.89 | −4.88 | −4.81 | • • • |
| 43140 | −2.48 | −2.46 | −3.80 | −3.88 | −4.58 | −4.71 | −4.82 | • • • |
| 43020 | −1.77 | −1.97 | −3.07 | −3.40 | −4.14 | −4.42 | −4.70 | • • • |
| 42900 | −1.06 | −1.42 | −2.37 | −2.87 | −3.61 | −4.00 | −4.41 | • • • |
| 42780 | −0.35 | −0.81 | −1.66 | −2.26 | −2.97 | −3.46 | −3.96 | • • • |

This handbook will help answer those questions. We discuss how
datasets are organized, how they are visualized and analyzed, and
how data organization can be changed to help in the analysis.

We supply details on the prevalent technical data format
standards, and how files in these specific formats can be read. If
you deal with technical data, these topics should help you
organize and understand your data. We set the stage by presenting
four more researchers and their data…

## Michael Astroe—FITS Data

**Figure I.2**
*FITS Image*

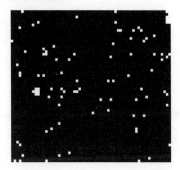

Mike Astroe's research is the Crab Nebula. He plans to use two images from a compact disc of data from the Einstein X-ray satellite: one image of the X-ray intensity, another image of the instrumental response. He needs to display the raw images, subtract background counts, eliminate noise, then visualize and analyze the modified images.

## Dr. Tim Boans—MRI Scans

**Figure I.3**
*Two MRI Scans*

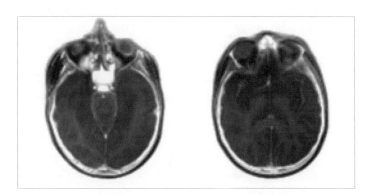

Dr. Boans has spent an afternoon taking a series of 2-dimensional MRI (magnetic resonance imaging) images of a colleague's head. He would like to combine these images in a way that reconstructs the head. Tim is wondering what is the best way to store these images, combine them, and visualize them as a single 3-dimensional object.

## Jeanne Beeker—Solubility Experiments

Jeanne is studying the solubility of various compounds in certain solvents. She has tested 72 compounds with six solvents, looking for interesting correlations between the solubility of the compounds with the solvents used. How can she analyze and graph her data to gain insight into this experiment?

*Figure I.4*
*Solubility Experiment*

|  | ETH | OCT | CCL4 | C6C6 | HEX | CHCL3 |
|---|---|---|---|---|---|---|
| METHANOL | -1.150 | -0.770 | -2.100 | -1.890 | -2.800 | -1.260 |
| ETHANOL | -0.570 | -0.310 | -1.400 | -1.620 | -2.100 | -0.850 |
| PROPANOL | -0.020 | 0.250 | -0.820 | -0.700 | -1.520 | -0.400 |
| BUTANOL | 0.890 | 0.880 | -0.400 | -0.120 | -0.700 | 0.450 |
| PENTANOL | 1.200 | 1.560 | 0.400 | 0.620 | -0.400 | 1.050 |
| HEXANOL | 1.800 | 2.030 | 0.990 | 1.300 | 0.460 | 1.690 |
| HEPTANOL | 2.400 | 2.410 | 1.670 | 1.910 | 1.010 | 2.410 |
| ACETIC_ACID | -0.340 | -0.170 | -2.450 | -2.260 | -3.060 | -1.600 |
| PROPIONIC_ACID | 0.270 | 0.330 | -1.600 | -1.350 | -2.140 | -0.960 |
| BUTYRIC_ACID | 0.610 | 0.790 | -0.970 | -0.960 | -1.760 | -0.270 |
| HEXANOIC_ACID | 1.950 | 1.920 | 0.570 | 0.300 | -0.460 | 1.150 |
| PENTANOIC_ACID | 1.000 | 1.390 | -0.420 | -0.100 | -1.000 | 0.280 |
| TRICHLOROACETIC_ACID | 1.210 | 1.330 | -1.660 | -1.300 | -2.630 | -0.690 |
| DICHLOROACETIC_ACID | 1.310 | 0.920 | -2.310 | -1.400 | -2.720 | -0.890 |
| CHLOROACETIC_ACID | 0.370 | 0.220 | -2.560 | -1.600 | -3.140 | -1.920 |
| METHYLACETATE | 0.430 | 0.180 | 0.320 | 0.530 | -0.260 | 1.160 |
| · | · | · | · | · | · | · |
| · | · | · | · | · | · | · |
| · | · | · | · | · | · | · |

## Wolfram Herth—Ground Water Information

Wolfram is looking at the groundwater level in a Texas county. He has recorded the latitude, longitude, surface elevation, and groundwater level at numerous sites across that county. Wolfram wants to visualize the data in a way that is clear to county commissioners and other policy makers. In addition, he needs to make sure that he has the most accurate possible model of the groundwater level, given the necessarily small number of measurements.

*Figure I.5*
*Groundwater Information*

| X DISTANCE | Y DISTANCE | LEVEL |
|---|---|---|
| 21843.750000 | 24086.339844 | -6.821851 |
| 21781.250000 | 24086.339844 | -6.849205 |
| 21812.500000 | 24032.210938 | -6.853322 |
| 21875.000000 | 24032.210938 | -6.827897 |
| 21812.500000 | 24140.462891 | -6.818563 |
| 21906.250000 | 24086.339844 | -6.794088 |
| 21875.000000 | 24140.462891 | -6.788042 |
| 21718.750000 | 24086.339844 | -6.875371 |
| 21750.000000 | 24140.462891 | -6.848110 |
| 21750.000000 | 24032.210938 | -6.878048 |
| 21781.250000 | 23978.089844 | -6.883172 |
| 21843.750000 | 23978.089844 | -6.859762 |
| 21906.250000 | 23978.089844 | -6.835976 |
| 21937.500000 | 24032.210938 | -6.802373 |
| 21781.250000 | 24194.589844 | -6.819032 |
| . | . | . |
| . | . | . |
| . | . | . |

## Important Questions to Answer

These scientists and engineers want to get as much information as they can out of their data, and they want to show other people the results. But before trying to graph or visualize the data, they need to know the answers to these questions:

### How Are the Numbers Stored?

Are the numbers in the datafile stored as *bytes*, as *integers*, as *fixed-point numbers*, as *floating point numbers*, or as *ASCII text numbers*? How much space do these numbers take up? What is the range and precision of those stored numbers?

### How Is the Data Organized?

Is the data organized as a *column* datafile, as a *2D matrix* datafile, a *3D matrix* datafile, or as a *polygonal* datafile? Is the data in a standard format? If so, what are the limitations of that format? What programs can best interpret that format?

### What Is the Dimensionality of the Data?

Which numbers are the actual *data values* such as temperature, and which are the *data locations,* such as distance or time? What is the *dimensionality* of the datafile (defined as the number of data locations)? Can the dimensionality of the datafile be modified to help analyze and visualize the graph?

### Is the Data on a Grid?

If the data is on a grid, is it a rectangular grid, a warped grid, or a completely unstructured grid? Is there a connectivity list defining the grid node points? Is the data defined at grid intersections or in the center of grid polygons?

## What Is the Best Way to Analyze the Data?

*The purpose of this handbook is to help any scientist or engineer answer these questions for his or her data.*

Perhaps the most important way to analyze data is by visualizing it, as line graphs, color images, contour plots, volumetric plots, etc. The best visualization techniques for a particular datafile depend strongly on the dimensionality of the data.

The answers to the questions for the five examples given above are discussed throughout the book, and are summarized in Part V.

# A Quick Tour of This Book

## The Data Handbook in Five Parts

PART I, INTRODUCTION, introduces five researchers and their data. Their problems and concerns with their data are examined throughout the book.

PART II, NUMBERS IN COMPUTERS, lists the ways data can be stored digitally (bytes, integers, floating point, ASCII text), discusses the advantages and disadvantages of each method, and presents some pitfalls of digital data storage.

PART III, THE DATA UNIVERSE, discusses in detail the organization of technical data. In particular, the concept of data dimensionality is stressed, and information is given on the storage, analysis, and visualization of column, 2D matrix, 3D matrix, and polygonal datafiles.

PART IV, DATA FORMATS, discusses standard data formats such as FITS, TIFF, DXF, netCDF, EPSF, SEG-Y, and ACR-NEMA. The HDF file format in particular is discussed in detail.

PART V, BRINGING IT ALL TOGETHER, gives answers to the questions posed above for our five researchers.

## Chapters in Part II, Numbers in Computers

Chapter 1, AN OVERVIEW OF NUMBERS IN COMPUTERS, defines what is meant by *data*, and how numbers are categorized as binary (*bytes, integers, floating point*) or text (*ASCII text*).

Chapter 2, BYTES, introduces fundamental concepts of digital data and discusses the storage of numbers as bytes.

Chapter 3, INTEGERS AND FIXED-POINT NUMBERS, discusses the storage of numbers as integers and as fixed-point numbers.

Chapter 4, FLOATING POINT NUMBERS, discusses the storage of numbers as single-precision or double-precision floating point.

Chapter 5, ASCII TEXT NUMBERS, discusses numbers as ASCII text strings, and how this differs fundamentally from binary.

## Chapters in Part III, The Data Universe

Chapter 6, A MAP OF THE DATA UNIVERSE, defines *data value*, *data location*, and *data dimensionality* and shows how datafiles are categorized as column, 2D matrix, 3D matrix and polygonal.

Chapter 7, COLUMN DATA, discusses the organization, storage, visualization, and dimensionality of column data.

Chapter 8, 2D MATRIX DATA, details the organization, storage, visualization, and the grids of 2D matrix data.

Chapter 9, 3D MATRIX (VOLUMETRIC) DATA, talks about the organization, storage, and the visualization of 3D matrix (volumetric) data.

Chapter 10, POLYGONAL DATA, discusses the organization, storage, visualization, and the grids of polygonal data.

Chapter 11, CONVERSIONS AND ADDING DIMENSIONS, details data conversions such as converting column to matrix data. Also discussed is the advantages of adding dimensions to your data for analysis and visualization.

## Chapters in Part IV, Data Formats

Chapter 12, DATA FORMATS, gives information on popular technical data file formats such as FITS, TIFF, DXF, netCDF, EPSF, SEG-Y, and ACR-NEMA.

Chapter 13, THE HDF STANDARD, goes into some detail about HDF, an emerging standard for storing and disseminating technical data.

## How to Use This Book

We hope that this book will be used as both a reference and as something to curl up with at night. For those of you using it as a reference, we have included the following navigational aids:

- A table of contents at the beginning of the book.
- An expanded table of contents at the beginning of each chapter.
- An index at the back.
- A glossary of key concepts and phrases.

For those of you interested in reading the book straight through, we offer the following suggestions:

- Study the five cases introduced in Part I. We refer to them often. Also, consider ways you use data in your work.
- Some of Part II is reference material and can be skipped without loss of continuity. This is particularly true of Chapter 4. We have tried to mark off material that easily can be skipped with the heading 'For Real Techies.'
- If you use ASCII text files to store your data, study Chapter 5 carefully.
- Chapter 6 is the most important in the book and should be studied in detail by everyone. All researchers should thoroughly understand data *dimensionality* to get the most out of their data.
- Chapters 7 and 8 should be read studiously by anyone with 2-dimensional data. In particular, it is important to understand how 2D matrix storage differs from column storage.
- Part V returns to the five cases that started the book, and should be read in its entirety.

# PART II
# NUMBERS IN COMPUTERS

*"...when you can measure what you are speaking
about, and express it in numbers, you know
something about it; but when you cannot measure it,
when you cannot express it in numbers, your
knowledge is of a meager & unsatisfactory kind."*

—William Thomson, Lord Kelvin

If you want a computer to analyze or graph your data, you must first
convert the data into numbers. Many scientists and engineers never
think about how a computer stores numbers, but the process of
digitizing data contains several potentially serious pitfalls. This
section, 'Numbers in Computers,' will help you avoid those traps.

The first chapter is an overview of numbers in computers. Chapters
2 through 5 detail the use of byte, integer, floating point, and
ASCII text number formats to store numbers in computers.

# CHAPTER 1
# AN OVERVIEW OF
# NUMBERS IN COMPUTERS

## Turning Data into Numbers

In this book we are concerned only with technical data that can be quantified or represented as numbers. Clearly, temperature measurements and calculations of wind speed can be expressed as numbers.

A city name, a color, or the name of a type of flower also can be expressed numerically—for example, the latitude and longitude of the town, the RGB values for the color, or an index number for the flower type.

**Figure 1.1**
*Turning Objects into Numbers*

| Object | Numerical Representation | Comments |
|---|---|---|
| Urbana, IL | 40° 36' N, 88° 12' W 39,000 Population | Cities can be quantified as locations, population, etc. |
| Purple | Red............21,853 Green..........1,303 Blue..........52,428 | Red, Green, Blue values (out of 65,536). Could also use Hue, Saturation, Intensity values. |
| Marigold | Flower Index #234 | An arbitrary flower number: perhaps numbers for genus and species could also be used. |

Can we quantify every type of data? Probably not. What numbers would you pick to represent a nice spring day? Surely your experience of that day contains information, but it is of a type not amenable to quantitative analysis. All the information in a poem (including subjective impressions created by the language use) also would be difficult to quantify.

**Figure 1.2**
*Quantifying a Phrase*

| Object | Numerical Representation | Comments |
|---|---|---|
| A nice spring day. | ? | Should we choose a 'nice day' index? This would not be fruitful. |

In any case, this handbook will discuss only data that can be converted easily into numbers. Apologies to all the poets out there.

## Storing Numbers on Computers

Computers have many ways of storing numbers, as the following exercise illustrates.

Exercise: What do the following items have in common?

```
332E3134313539323635h
             40490FDBh
   400921FB54442D18h
                    3
                  11b
           '3.14159265'
                   'π'
```

Each item is a particular computer representation of π. A brief description of each line is given in Figure 1.3.

*Figure 1.3*
*Representations*
*of π*

| | |
|---|---|
| 332E3134313539323635h | Hex listing of the ASCII text string '3.141259265' |
| 40490FDBh | Hex listing of the single-precision floating point representation of π |
| 400921FB54442D18h | Hex listing of the double-precision floating point representation of π |
| 3 | Value of π as stored in an integer |
| 11b | Binary representation of that integer |
| '3.14159265' | Text of the ASCII string |
| 'π' | Symbolic representation of π |

More detailed discussions of each line in this exercise will be given in the appropriate places in the following four chapters.

You may wonder what the point is; if you don't worry about how your car works, why should you need to care how a computer stores numbers? If you have ever flooded a car engine, you probably know that a little knowledge about fuel-air mixtures can come in handy. You will find that a moderate understanding of computerized numbers will pay dividends again and again.

## Binary Numbers and ASCII Text Numbers

Computers store numbers in two fundamental ways, known as *binary number* storage and *ASCII text number* storage. This is the most important concept in the computer storage of numbers.

| | |
|---|---|
| Binary Numbers | Bytes, integers, floating point |
| | Fixed precision |
| | Efficient |
| | Not human readable |
| ASCII Text Numbers | Text, characters, ASCII |
| | Variable precision |
| | Not efficient |
| | Human readable |

There are three types of binary numbers: *bytes*, *integers*, and *floating point numbers*. Every binary number is stored in a fixed amount of space with a fixed range of values and a fixed precision. The numbers are coded in a very efficient way that is not 'human readable,' meaning that printing the file will produce garbage. Binary data is meant to be read only by computer programs. Chapters 2, 3, and 4 discuss the three binary number formats in detail.

ASCII text numbers are text strings, the same format used for conventional written material. Each ASCII text number uses a variable amount of space (one character or byte per decimal digit), has a variable range of values, a variable precision, and is human readable. Chapter 5 discusses ASCII text numbers in depth.

## Evaluating Number Formats

When evaluating these formats for the storage of your data, it is useful to keep the following questions in mind.

- How exactly is the number format stored on the computer?
- How expensive is it in terms of disk space and CPU usage?
- What is the maximum range of values (from smallest to largest number) you can store with the number format?
- What is the numerical precision (smallest difference between two values) of the number format?
- What are the problems associated with doing calculations with the number format?
- How easy is it to move datafiles written with a particular number format between dissimilar computers?

Chapters 2, 3, 4, and 5 each summarize the answers to these questions for a particular number format.

# CHAPTER 2
# BYTE NUMBERS

## Bits and Bytes

| Binary Numbers | Base-2 with digits of either 0 or 1 |
|---|---|
| Decimal Numbers | Base-10 with digits of 0 — 9, inclusive |

Computers store everything as *bits*; each bit has a value of either 0 or 1. (*Bit* is a contraction for <u>bi</u>nary digi<u>t</u>.) Every normal computer deals not with these bits but with combinations of eight bits called a *byte*. One bit can represent two values (0 and 1), two bits can represent four values (00, 01, 10, 11), and the eight bits of a byte can represent 256, or $2^8$, distinct values.

Recall that in decimal numbers (*decimal* meaning base 10) the right-most column of a multi-digit number is for the 1s ($10^0$) column, the column to the left of that represents the number of 10s ($10^1$), and then there is a column for the 100s ($10^2$), etc. In binary numbers (*binary* meaning base 2), the columns are for 1s ($2^0$), then 2s ($2^1$), and then 4s ($2^2$), etc. Just as eight decimal digits will give you $10^8$ unique values, eight binary digits will give you $2^8$ or 256 unique values.

**Figure 2.1**
*Decimal Places and Binary Places*

| Place | 8th | 7th | 6th | 5th | 4th | 3rd | 2nd | 1st |
|---|---|---|---|---|---|---|---|---|
| *Decimal* | $10^7$ | $10^6$ | $10^5$ | $10^4$ | $10^3$ | $10^2$ | $10^1$ | $10^0$ |
| | 10 million | 1 million | 100,000 | 10,000 | 1,000 | 100 | 10 | 1 |
| *Binary* | $2^7$ | $2^6$ | $2^5$ | $2^4$ | $2^3$ | $2^2$ | $2^1$ | $2^0$ |
| | 128 | 64 | 32 | 16 | 8 | 4 | 2 | 1 |

A valid decimal number might be 179, which means $1 \times 100 + 7 \times 10 + 9 \times 1$. A valid binary number might be 10110011, which means $1 \times 128 + 1 \times 32 + 1 \times 16 + 1 \times 2 + 1 \times 1$. The same value is represented by 179 in *decimal* and 10110011 in *binary*.

**Figure 2.2**
*How to Represent 179*

| Representation | What it Means |
|---|---|
| 179 decimal | $1 \times 100 + 7 \times 10 + 9 \times 1$ |
| 10110011 binary | $1 \times 128 + 1 \times 32 + 1 \times 16 + 1 \times 2 + 1 \times 1$ |

The terms *binary number* and *decimal number* tell you only how the numbers are displayed (in base-2 digits or base-10 digits). The terms tell you nothing about the actual values they represent.

## Unsigned Bytes

It is natural to use bytes to represent numbers. Typically the number 0 will map to the binary number 00000000b (the b is for *binary*), the number 1 to 00000001b, the number 2 to 00000010b, and the number 255 to 11111111b. This particular mapping of numbers to binary representations is called *unsigned,* for reasons that soon should become clear.

**Figure 2.3**
*Unsigned Bytes*

| Value | Binary |
|-------|-----------|
| 0 | 0000 0000b |
| 1 | 0000 0001b |
| 127 | 0111 1111b |
| 128 | 1000 0000b |
| 254 | 1111 1110b |
| 255 | 1111 1111b |

The value stored in a byte could be displayed as the decimal equivalent of the number (left column in Figure 2.3), or as the binary representation (right column). Note that in this book all binary numbers will end in b. There are numerous other conventions. As shown in Figure 2.4, all eight bits of the unsigned byte are used to represent a value.

**Figure 2.4**
*Unsigned Byte*

*Value*

| 8 bits |
|--------|

## Signed Bytes

How do computers store negative numbers? Recall that a byte can store 256 unique values. There is no reason why those values have to be 0 to 255 inclusive—they can be -128 to 127 instead. By convention, *signed bytes* have the mapping of values to binary representations shown in Figures 2.5 and 2.6.

**Figure 2.5**
*Signed Bytes*

| Value | Binary |
|---|---|
| -128 | 1000 0000b |
| -127 | 1000 0001b |
| -1 | 1111 1111b |
| 0 | 0000 0000b |
| 1 | 0000 0001b |
| 127 | 0111 1111b |

Figure 2.6 shows that in signed bytes, one bit is used to represent the *sign* ('s' here), and seven bits are used to represent the *value*. This convention has two useful properties. First, the initial (top) bit is set to 1 for all negative numbers. (This bit is often called the *sign bit*.) Second, the representation of numbers between 0 and 127 is the same for *signed* and *unsigned* integers.

**Figure 2.6**
*Signed Byte*

| s | Value |
|---|---|
| 1 | 7 bits |

To change the sign of a stored number you 'flip' all of the bits (0s to 1s, 1s to 0s), and then *add* 1. You can see this clearly in Figure 2.7. This convention is called *twos-complement*.

**Figure 2.7**
*Twos-Complement*

| Value | Binary |
|---|---|
| -127 | 1000 0001b |
| 127 | 0111 1111b |

There is no way to tell by looking at the bits whether an integer is signed. You (or your program) just must know. (Compare unsigned 128 in Figure 2.3 with signed -128 in Figure 2.5.)

*Be sure you always know whether your integers are signed or unsigned.*

*Michael Astroe used an early version of Spyglass Transform to look at his FITS files. That version of the software assumed that FITS images consist of unsigned integers. In fact, his values were all signed, so all of the negative values were interpreted as large positive values, making a mess of his images. (Transform now checks for signed FITS files.)*

## Twos-Complement vs. Ones-Complement

Most computers currently use twos-complement arithmetic as described above, but back in the computational stone ages, machines such as the Control Data Cybers used *ones-complement* arithmetic. In ones-complement, to change the sign of a stored number you just flip all of the bits. No 'add by 1.'

*Ask an old Cyber programmer about negative zero. Carefully.*

This was thought to be more efficient, but it created a problem— now there were two representations for zero: 00000000b and 11111111b. Programs had to check for 'positive' zero and also for 'negative' zero (!).

## Hexadecimal Representation

We have discussed two ways of displaying numbers: decimal numbers and binary numbers. Binary number representations are handy because you can see what bits are set, but binary numbers can get very large and clumsy. What would be nice is a compact representation of the binary representation of your numbers. Such a format exists, and it is called *hex*.

 In hex (short for <u>hex</u>adecimal, or base 16) , each byte is divided into two 4-bit chunks (sometimes called *nibbles* or *nybbles*), and each 4-bit chunk is displayed as a number. Since 4 bits can represent 16 separate values ($2^4$), each hex number is between 0 and 15. For example, the number 156 would be equal to 9,12 in hex.

However, you will never see hex written that way. By convention, the numbers 10 through 15 are labelled A through F, so 156 is displayed as 9C in hex, or 9Ch (where the *h* is for *hexadecimal*). In this book, all hex numbers will have h appended.

**Figure 2.8**
*Different Representations of 156*

| Decimal | 156 |
|---|---|
| Binary | 1001 1100b |
| PseudoHex | 9,12 |
| Hex | 9Ch |

There are always two hex digits for every byte of data. Sometimes hex numbers are displayed as $9C or 0 × 9C instead of 9Ch.

Figure 2.9 shows the equivalence of decimal, hex, and binary numbers up to 15.

**Figure 2.9**
*Hex Numbers*

| Decimal | Hex | Binary |
|---------|-----|--------|
| 0 | 0 | 0000 |
| 1 | 1 | 0001 |
| 2 | 2 | 0010 |
| 3 | 3 | 0011 |
| 4 | 4 | 0100 |
| 5 | 5 | 0101 |
| 6 | 6 | 0110 |
| 7 | 7 | 0111 |
| 8 | 8 | 1000 |
| 9 | 9 | 1001 |
| 10 | A | 1010 |
| 11 | B | 1011 |
| 12 | C | 1100 |
| 13 | D | 1101 |
| 14 | E | 1110 |
| 15 | F | 1111 |

*(Figure 2.9 — Hex Numbers)*

Figure 2.10 shows the hex values for the unsigned bytes we presented earlier.

**Figure 2.10**
*Hex Values for*
*Unsigned Bytes*

| Value | Hex | Binary |
|-------|-----|--------|
| 0 | 00h | 0000 0000b |
| 1 | 01h | 0000 0001b |
| 127 | 7Fh | 0111 1111b |
| 128 | 80h | 1000 0000b |
| 254 | FEh | 1111 1110b |
| 255 | FFh | 1111 1111b |

Figure 2.11 shows the hex values for the *signed* bytes we presented earlier.

**Figure 2.11**
*Hex Values for Signed Bytes*

| Value | Hex | Binary |
|-------|-----|--------|
| −128 | 40h | 1000 0000b |
| −127 | 41h | 1000 0001b |
| −1 | FFh | 1111 1111b |
| 0 | 00h | 0000 0000b |
| 1 | 01h | 0000 0001b |
| 127 | 3Fh | 0111 1111b |

## Octal Numbers

You also may see *octal* representations of numbers (base 8). Octal digits range from 0 to 7, and each octal digit represents three bits. Therefore, the octal representation for 9Ch is 234o (o for octal). Octal representation is not widely used since octal requires three digits to represent a byte; hex requires just two digits.

## Kilobytes and Megabytes

*If you need to worry about the exact number of bytes your disk files take up, you need a bigger disk drive.*

Disk file sizes are often expressed in *kilobytes* and *megabytes*. A file may be listed as taking 32 kilobytes, or 32K bytes. This does not mean exactly 32,000 bytes. A kilobyte is defined as $2^{10}$ bytes, or 1024 bytes. So 32K bytes is actually equal to 32 x 1024 or 32,768 bytes.

A megabyte is correspondingly defined as $2^{20}$ bytes, or 1,048,576 bytes. Therefore, 32 megabytes ( 32M bytes) equals 33,554,432 bytes.

## Byte Numbers: Advantages & Pitfalls

### Computational Resources

Byte data makes very efficient use of disk space, and for many computers,[*] calculations with bytes are much quicker than for other types of number storage. However…

### Range of Values

Bytes are rarely used for the storage of technical information because your numbers must be either in the range 0 to 255 for unsigned bytes or -128 to 127 for signed bytes. The one function for which byte storage of information is popular is the storage of image data, discussed in more detail in Chapter 12.

### Numerical Precision

*Numerical precision* is defined here as the smallest difference between two values stored in a particular format. For byte numbers, precision is always one (1).

---

[*] Not true for Cray computers, which deal with data in 64-bit chunks only.

## Calculations with Bytes

Doing calculations with byte data is very dangerous, since it is easy to exceed the range of values. See Chapter 3 for a discussion on integer calculations.

## Portability

*When moving byte, integer, or floating-point files between computers, make sure you are doing a binary transfer. For example, enter* `set file type binary` *when using Kermit, or enter* `bin` *when using FTP.*

All popular computers store signed and unsigned bytes in the same way, which is an advantage. However, you must know whether your bytes are signed or unsigned, since there is absolutely no way to know by looking at the data.

Some file transfer programs will, by default, throw away the first bit of every byte. You must explicitly tell the program to transfer all eight bits.  Also, you must set the transfer mode to `binary`. See Chapter 5 on ASCII numbers for more information on file transfers.

## Summary

Figure 2.12 summarizes the attributes of byte numbers.

**Figure 2.12**
*Bytes Summary*

| Attribute | Rating |
|---|---|
| Computational Resources | Efficient |
| Range of Values | Poor |
| Numerical Precision | Poor |
| Calculation Considerations | Dangerous |
| Portability | Excellent |

This table will be expanded in each of the next three chapters as another type of number storage is added to the consideration.

# CHAPTER 3
# INTEGERS AND FIXED-POINT NUMBERS

## Short Integers and Long Integers

The obvious way to store a number larger than $255$ is to use two bytes. This gives $2^{16}$ or 65,536 possible values. This 2-byte number is called an *integer* (or *short integer*). It takes four hex digits to display the values in a short integer.

**Figure 3.1**
*Unsigned Short Integer*

$$Value$$
| 16 bits |
|---|

For even larger numbers, the idea extends naturally.

**Figure 3.2**
*Unsigned Long Integer*

$$Value$$
| 32 bits |
|---|

Note that using *short* and *long* to refer to 2-byte and 4-byte integers is common but by no means universal. Figure 3.3 is the table of ranges for unsigned integers.

**Figure 3.3**
*Ranges for Unsigned Integers*

| Type | Bytes | Range of Values |
|---|---|---|
| Unsigned Byte | 1 | 0 to 255 |
| Unsigned Short Integer | 2 | 0 to 65,536 |
| Unsigned Long Integer | 4 | 0 to 4,294,967,296 |
| Unsigned 64-bit Integer | 8 | 0 to $1.84467 \times 10^{19}$ |

All computers support short integers and most support long integers. Support for 64-bit integers is rare; such large values are usually stored in floating point numbers, described in the Chapter 4.

The concept of signed bytes extends naturally to integers with two bytes...

**Figure 3.4**
*Signed Short Integer*

| s | Value |
|---|---|
| 1 | 15 bits |

and to integers with four or eight bytes.

**Figure 3.5**
*Signed Long Integer*

| s | Value |
|---|---|
| 1 | 31 bits |

Below is the table of ranges for signed integers. Compare this table with Figure 3.3. In most computers, bytes are unsigned but all other integers are signed. There are exceptions.

**Figure 3.6**
*Ranges for Signed Integers*

| Type | Bytes | Range of Values |
|---|---|---|
| Signed Byte | 1 | -128 to 127 |
| Signed Short Integer | 2 | -32768 to 32767 |
| Signed Long Integer | 4 | -2,147,483,648 to 2,147,483,647 |
| Signed 64-bit Integer | 8 | $-9.2234 \times 10^{18}$ to $9.2234 \times 10^{18}$ |

## Fixed-Point Numbers

What size integer should you use to store your values? The quick answer is to use the smallest type that will store the largest value you will ever deal with. If you are willing to *scale* your values before you store them, however, you will need a longer answer.

*For example, **Wolfram Herth** wants to store surface elevations. The highest possible value for elevation is Mt. Everest at ≈29,000 feet, so his best choice might be to store elevation as an unsigned short integer. However, his elevation data has better than one-foot precision, so he can multiply his measured values (734.598 ft, for example) by 100,000 and stored the results (in this example, 73,459,800) in an unsigned long integer. He must remember to divide by 100,000 before displaying his values.*

In Figure 3.7 the number stored in the computer is equal to the *multiplier* times the actual value. *Precision* is the inverse of the multiplier.

**Figure 3.7**
*Ways to Store Everest Altitude in a Fixed-Point Number*

| Type | Multiplier | Range | Precision |
|---|---|---|---|
| Unsigned Byte | .005 | 0 to 51,000 | 200 ft |
| Unsigned Short Integer | 1 | 0 to 65,536 | 1 ft |
| Unsigned Long Integer | 100,000 | 0 to 42,949.67296 | 0.00012 in |

This type of bookkeeping is called *fixed-point arithmetic* because the position of the decimal <u>point</u> stays <u>fixed</u>. The equation is

$$y = m \times x$$

where $y$ is the actual stored value, $m$ is the multiplier, and $x$ is the original value. The largest number you can store will be $(2^N-1)/m$, where $N$ is the number of bits in the integer (if you are using *unsigned* integers). The *precision* (difference between two adjacent values) will be $1/m$.

## Offset Values

In special cases, you may consider adding an *offset* value to your data before storing it. You can use offsets to increase the precision of your calculation at the expense of the maximum range of values. The equation for storing a number with offsets is

$$y = m \times (x + b)$$

where $b$ is the offset. For example, if you wanted to store a value that is always between 30 and 40 in a byte, you could set $b = -30$ and $m = 256/10 = 25.6$. In this way your stored values will have an accuracy of $1/m = .039$, much better than the precision of 1 that you would have without any conversion, and better than the precision of $40/256 = .156$ that you would have without the offset.

Note that for the unsigned byte example above, the multiplier of .005 cannot be represented using integer numbers. So instead of multiplying your data by .005 before storing it, you could divide the data by 200, which is an integer. Typically, however, people will use floating point arithmetic to do such conversions.

*There are two types of fixed-point users: those who have messed up because of the multiplier or the precision, and those who will.*

You must be careful when using fixed-point numbers, because it is easy to forget those multipliers or to forget your precision.

*For example, **Dr. Tim Boans'** MRI image datafiles represent the intensity at every point with 12 bits. Tim wanted to save some disk space, so he scaled his 12-bit intensities (0 to 4095) to 8-bit values (0 to 255) that can be stored in single bytes. However, Dr. Boans was caught short when he had trouble making out the boundaries of an indistinct shape on the image. Changing the contrast on the 8-bit image just made it 'noiser.'*

*Tim then decided to store the full intensity range for each datapoint in a 16-bit short integer. This doubled the disk space used, but when he changed the contrast on his 12-bit image, the shape boundaries were very distinct.*

## Range of Values

When using integers, you must always be aware of the maximum range for the selected integer type, and whether the integer is signed or unsigned. If you try to store as an integer a number that is outside the allowed range, unfortunate results may occur.

*Try to store 40,000 as a signed short integer. Print the result. If you are lucky, your computer will complain. If you are unlucky, you will get -25536.*

The problem becomes more acute for fixed-point numbers, especially if you have an offset value. You must be very careful when selecting the multiplier and offset to make sure that any value you plan to store in that number will never exceed the maximum scaled range. [*]

## Numerical Precision

You must always be aware of the information that is lost when you use integers or fixed-point numbers. For example, whenever you store data in integers you necessarily discard the fractional part of the data.  With fixed-point numbers,  you throw away the part of your number that is more accurate than the inverse of the multiplier.

## Calculations

You must be careful *not* to exceed the maximum range of values when using integers and fixed-point numbers. This concern becomes even more acute when you do calculations. For example, two height data values of 25,000 and 15,000 are individually inside the allowed signed short integer range, but their sum is *not*.

---

[*] The minimum scaled value $x_{min} = y_{min}/m - b$ and the maximum scaled value $x_{max} = y_{max}/m - b$, where x is the original value, y is the actual stored value, m is the multiplier, and b is the offset.

---

**Figure 3.8**
*Sample Exercise #1*

Exercise: You want the average of ten height values. Assume all variables are signed short integers, and all height values are around 10,000. Will this program work?

```
      INTEGER*2  SUM,AVERAGE,HEIGHT(10)
      SUM = 0
      DO 10 I = 1,10
          SUM = SUM + HEIGHT(I)
10    CONTINUE
      AVERAGE = SUM / 10
```

The program in Figure 3.8 yields a useless answer because the value stored in SUM rapidly exceeds the maximum allowable value, even though the value stored in AVERAGE does not.

**Figure 3.9**
*Sample Exercise #2*

Exercise: Is this program any better?

```
      INTEGER*2 AVERAGE,HEIGHT(10)
      AVERAGE = 0
      DO 10 I=1,10
          AVERAGE = AVERAGE + HEIGHT(I)/10
10    CONTINUE
```

The value stored in AVERAGE never exceeds the maximum allowable range, but there is a problem. You throw away the last digit in every HEIGHT value, which means that your AVERAGE value could be off by as much as 9 feet!

## Truncation Error

This type of problem is called *truncation error*, since most computers truncate the result of the division of one integer by another. When a result is truncated, the fractional part is thrown away. The alternative is *rounding*, up or down.

**Figure 3.10**
*Divisors and Results*

| Data | Divisor | Result | Type of Division |
|------|---------|--------|------------------|
| 50 | 10 | 5 | truncation & rounding |
| 54 | 10 | 5 | truncation & rounding |
| 55 | 10 | 5 | truncation |
| 55 | 10 | 6 | rounding |
| 59 | 10 | 5 | truncation |
| 59 | 10 | 6 | rounding |

*Complicated fixed-point arithmetic should only be used when raw speed is more important than maintainability, validity, and sanity.*

If you are doing calculations using fixed-point numbers, you must be especially careful. Imagine, for example, keeping track of the maximum allowed ranges and accuracy concerns when all of your variables have offsets and multipliers. Guaranteeing the correctness of such calculations is not for the faint of heart.

Figure 3.11 consists of C versions of Figures 3.8 and 3.9.

**Figure 3.11**
*C Program Segments*

```
C Segment #1
     signed short height[9],average,sum,i;
     for (i=0; i<=9; i++)
        sum += height[i];
     average = sum/10;

C Segment #2
     signed short height[9],average,i;
     for (i=0; i<=9; i++)
        average += height[i]/10;
```

## Calculations: The Right Way

*Number formats for calculations should have a larger range of values than the formats used for data storage (integers for byte data, floating-point for long integer data, etc.).*

How can you calculate with integers and fixed-point numbers? The safe way is to use number formats that have a much larger range of values than the format you use to store your data. For example, calculate byte data with short integers, and calculate short integer data with long integers. You could also use floating point numbers, discussed in Chapter 4.

So in Figure 3.8, defining SUM as a signed long integer would fix the problem. (However, the truncation problem shown in Figure 3.9 is *not* solved by defining AVERAGE as a long integer. )

# Byte Order

*Dr. Tim Boans has now changed his MRI images so each datapoint is a short integer (16 bits). He tries to open it with Spyglass Transform, carefully defining the file type as short integer, and giving the correct dimensions. The first time he gets garbage. He then discovers that if he skips the first byte of the file, an image appears. The image is strange, however, with lots of 'noise.' What is going on?*

He is being hit with a *byte order* problem. Remember that bits in bytes are ordered from the *most significant bit* on the left to the *least significant bit* on the right—the same way everyday decimal numbers are ordered, from most significant digit to least significant digit. In the number 156, for example, the 1 (on the left) is the most significant (100s place) and the 6 (on the right) the least significant (1s place).

Most computers follow the same pattern when ordering bytes for short and long integers: the *most significant byte* comes first, the *least significant byte* comes last. This is summarized in Figure 3.12, where $M$ stands for $2^{20} \approx 1$ million, $K$ for $2^{10} \approx 1$ thousand.

**Figure 3.12**
*Normal Byte Ordering*

| Byte  Position | 1 | 2 | 3 | 4 |
|---|---|---|---|---|
| Multiplier | 16M | 65K | 256 | 1 |
|  | $2^{24}$ | $2^{16}$ | $2^8$ | $2^0$ |

Two important computers do *not* order bytes this way:  The Digital Equipment Corporation VAX and the 80X86 (MS-DOS) computer. For both of these computers, the *least* significant byte comes *first*, but in slightly different ways. In the VAX, every two bytes are swapped. In the 80X86 computer, the entire four bytes are swapped end for end, as shown in Figure 3.13.

**Figure 3.13**
*Intel 80X86 Byte Ordering*

| Byte  Position | 1 | 2 | 3 | 4 |
|---|---|---|---|---|
| Multiplier | 1 | 256 | 65K | 16M |
|  | $2^0$ | $2^8$ | $2^{16}$ | $2^{24}$ |

If we represent the components of a long integer with A for the most significant byte and D for the least significant , the situation is as shown in Figure 3.14.

**Figure 3.14**
*Different Byte Orderings*

| IEEE Byte Ordering | A B C D |
|---|---|
| 8086 (MS-DOS) Byte Ordering | D C B A |
| VAX Byte Ordering | B A D C |

If you always use only one type of computer, byte order should never concern you. But if you move data between computers, this difference may 'come out to byte you.'

Now let's return to **Dr. Boans**. If his scanner used the normal byte order, his datafile would look like Figure 3.15.

**Figure 3.15**
*Normal Byte Order Integer File*

| MSB–1 | LSB–1 | MSB–2 | LSB–2 | MSB–3 | LSB–3 | MSB–4 | LSB–4 |
| --- | --- | --- | --- | --- | --- | --- | --- |

Here `MSB-1` means the most significant byte for the first integer, `LSB-1` means the least significant byte for the first integer, etc. Normally these two bytes would be read in pairs, as suggested by the pairings above. Unfortunately, Tim's scanner stores the bytes in reverse order, so his datafile actually looks like the following:

**Figure 3.16**
*Byte Swapped Order Integer File*

| LSB–1 | MSB–1 | LSB–2 | MSB–2 | LSB–3 | MSB–3 | LSB–4 | MSB–4 |
| --- | --- | --- | --- | --- | --- | --- | --- |

The Spyglass program Transform tried to interpret the least significant byte as the *most* significant, producing garbage. The second time Dr. Boans read the file he decided to try skipping the first byte; he read integer pairs as shown in Figure 3.17.

**Figure 3.17**
*Byte Swapped Order Integer File, Skipping first Byte*

| LSB–1 | MSB–1 | LSB–2 | MSB–2 | LSB–3 | MSB–3 | LSB–4 | MSB–4 |
| --- | --- | --- | --- | --- | --- | --- | --- |

Note that he is properly interpreting each 'most significant byte' *as* a most significant byte. However, each datapoint reads the least significant byte *from the following number*! This is why his image seemed 'noisy.' The solution to his problem is *not* to skip the first byte, but to use the 'Swap Bytes' option under Import in Transform.

## Integers and Fixed-Point: Advantages & Pitfalls

All computers love integers. Integers take little storage space, are very efficient, and contain none of the subtle surprises that floating point numbers have (as you will see in Chapter 4). Numbers that are naturally integers (index numbers, number of people, etc.) should be stored as integers.

### Computational Resources

Integer and fixed-point data are relatively frugal of disk space, and for many computers calculations with integers are much quicker than those using floating point numbers. This advantage is especially important for personal computers that do not have floating point coprocessors.

## Range of Values

A big problem with integers and fixed-point numbers is the ease with which you can exceed the maximum data range. You must be make absolutely sure you know whether your integers are signed or unsigned, and exactly what the maximum range of values is.

*Figure 3.18*
*Range of Values*

| Unsigned Byte | 0 to 255 |
|---|---|
| Signed Byte | -128 to 127 |
| Unsigned Short Integer | 0 to 65535 |
| Signed Short Integer | -32768 to 32767 |
| Signed Long Integer | $-2.14748 \times 10^9$ to $2.14748 \times 10^9$ |
| Signed 64-bit Integer | $-9.2234 \times 10^{18}$ to $9.2234 \times 10^{18}$ |
| Scaled Signed Short Integer* | -32768/m to 32767/m |
| Scaled Signed Short Integer * | $-2.147 \times 10^9$/m to $-2.147 \times 10^9$/m |

## Numerical Precision

With integers your numerical precision is always one. With fixed-point numbers, your precision is the inverse of the multiplier. In either case, you can always know what information you are saving and what information you are throwing away. For example, storing 3256.456 in an integer means you save 3256 and throw away 0.456. This explicitness is a big bonus.

*Figure 3.19*
*Numerical Precision*

| Byte, Short and Long Integer | 1 |
|---|---|
| Scaled Integer* | 1/m |

## Calculations with Integers

Doing calculations with integer data is dangerous, since it is easy to exceed the range of values. You can also introduce significant error if your work involves many calculations, since the truncation error is cumulative.

---

* Where m is the multiplier.

---

## Portability

Because of byte order problems, it is often difficult to transfer integer files between computers. (Though as shown in the Boans example, Spyglass Transform can swap bytes appropriately for files imported from VAXes and MS-DOS computers.)

Note that—especially for fixed-point numbers—you must know how the numbers are stored, their multipliers, and the offsets. The data itself does not contain this information. In other words, integer and fixed-point datafiles are not *self-describing*.

You must make sure that you set your file transfer program for a `binary` transfer when moving integer files between computers (as you must do for all binary data formats).

## Summary

*Figure 3.20*
*Comparision : Bytes with*
*Integers and Fixed-Point*

|  | *Bytes* | *Integers and Fixed-Point* |
|---|---|---|
| Computational Resources | Efficient | Efficient |
| Range of Values | Poor | Good |
| Numerical Precision | Poor | Good |
| Calculation Considerations | Dangerous | Be Careful |
| Portability | Excellent | Good |

The attributes of integers and fixed-point numbers have been added to the table.

# CHAPTER 4.
# FLOATING POINT NUMBERS

## Floating Point Numbers—Introduction

Floating point storage of data takes care of many of the nasty problems that occur when you are using integers and fixed-point numbers. But floating point storage has its own problems.

Suppose you want to store the value of π and think that 3 is not accurate enough. You could use *fixed-point arithmetic*: multiplying π by 100,000, storing the result (314159), and when printing it out remember to divide by 100,000. But for some types of data, fixed-point arithmetic just cannot work, as the exercise below shows.

**Figure 4.1**
*Example: Fixed-Point Limitations*

> The mass of an electron is $9.10956 \times 10^{-28}$g. Use fixed point arithmetic to store this number by multiplying it by 100,000 and saving it in an integer. Print the result. You should see 0.

The number $9.10956 \times 10^{-28}$ is displayed in *exponential notation*, which consists of a *fraction* (9.10956) and an *exponent*, or the 'power of 10' (-28). Although $910.956 \times 10^{-30}$ represents the same value as $9.10956 \times 10^{-28}$, by convention the fraction is usually between 1.0 and 9.999.

When you do not know the range of the data before performing the calculation, you may not know what the best multiplier is. One way around this problem is to store the fractional part of the number (9.10956) as a fixed-point number (910956), and then also store the exponent as an integer (-28). This should work for all numbers, as long as you express them in exponential notation first.

## Single-Precision Floating Point

Exponential notation is, in fact, the way floating point numbers are stored in computers. Each value is stored as two *signed* integers:  one for the fractional part, and one for the exponent. For example, the *IEEE Standard 754* format for 32-bit floating point numbers is shown in Figure 4.2. This format is usually called *single-precision floating point*, or *single-precision real*. It is called *floating point* because the decimal <u>point</u> <u>floats</u> (moves) based on the value of the exponent.

**Figure 4.2**
*IEEE Standard Single-Precision Float*

| s | exponent | fraction |
|---|----------|----------|
| 1 | 8 bits | 23 bits |

The first bit (labeled here with an $s$) is the sign bit: it is equal to $1$ for negative numbers, and $0$ for positive numbers. The next eight bits are used to store the *exponent*, and the final 23 bits to store the *fraction*. In our example, the sign bit might be $0$ (for a positive number), the exponent might be $-28$ (for $10^{-28}$), and the fractional part might equal $910956$.

**Figure 4.3**
*Possible Decimal Floating Point Representation of* $9.10956 \times 10^{-28}$

| s | exponent | fraction |
|---|----------|----------|
| 0 | $-28$ | 910956 |

Unfortunately, life is not that simple. Instead of storing the exponent and fraction of the *decimal* exponential representation of a value ($910956$ and $-28$ in our example of $9.10956 \times 10^{-28}$), the exponent and fraction of the *binary* exponential representation of a value are stored instead. The value $9.10956 \times 10^{-28}$ can be shown in binary notation as $1.1277089 \times 2^{-90}$, or more properly, $1.001000001011000110001b \times 2^{-1011010b}$. These two binary numbers, the fractional part and the exponent part, are actually stored in the number.

**Figure 4.4**
*Possible Binary Floating Point Representation of* $9.10956 \times 10^{-28}$

| s | exponent | fraction |
|---|----------|----------|
| 0 | $-90$ | 112771 |
| 0 | $-1011010b$ | 1001000001011000110001b |

Figure 4.4 still is not completely correct, but we are getting closer to the way floating point numbers are represented on computers.

*For Real Techies...*

## Binary Fractional Numbers

First, take a minute to consider what it means to write a number like $1.001000b$, a *binary fractional number*. Recall that in decimal numbers the right-most column to the left of the decimal point is for the $1$s ($10^0$) column, the next one to the left is the number of $10$s ($10^1$), etc.

Correspondingly, the left-most column to the right of the decimal point for decimal numbers is the $1/10$s ($10^{-1}$) column, etc. The situation is exactly analogous for binary numbers, where the columns represent the $1/2$, $1/4$, $1/8$, etc., values.

**Figure 4.5**
*Decimal and Binary Number Formats*

| Place | -1 | -2 | -3 | -4 | -5 | -6 |
|---|---|---|---|---|---|---|
| Decimal | $10^{-1}$ | $10^{-2}$ | $10^{-3}$ | $10^{-4}$ | $10^{-5}$ | $10^{-6}$ |
| | .1 | .01 | .001 | .0001 | .00001 | .000001 |
| Binary | $2^{-1}$ | $2^{-2}$ | $2^{-3}$ | $2^{-4}$ | $2^{-5}$ | $2^{-6}$ |
| | 1/2 | 1/4th | 1/8th | 1/16th | 1/32nd | 1/64th |

A valid *decimal  fractional number* might be 1.8125, which means $1 \times 1 + 8 \times 0.1 + 1 \times 0.01 + 2 \times 0.001 + 5 \times 0.0001$. A valid *binary fractional number* might be 1.1101b, which means $1 \times 1 + 1 \times (1/2) + 1 \times (1/4) + 1 \times (1/16)$. Both 1.8125 in *decimal* and 1.1101b in *binary* represent the same value.

**Figure 4.6**
*Binary and Decimal Fractions Decoded*

| Representation | What it Means |
|---|---|
| 1.8125 | $1 \times 1 + 8 \times 0.1 + 1 \times 0.01 + 2 \times 0.001 + 5 \times 0.0001$ |
| 1.1101b | $1 \times 1 + 1 \times (1/2) + 1 \times (1/4) + 1 \times (1/16)$ |

This exercise is not entirely academic: the fact that fractional numbers are stored as binary and not decimal fractions has implications for the numerical precision of your data. For example, 4.537 can be represented exactly as a decimal fractional number, but cannot be represented exactly as a binary fractional number. You may get 4.53699 instead.

*For Real Techies...*

## Decoding a Floating Point Number

It is very instructive to decode a floating point number, not because you will ever need to do this, but because it gives insight into the limitations of floating point numbers.

The quiz in Chapter 1 listed various representations of $\pi$. The second entry was 40490FDBh, which is the IEEE 32-bit single-precision representation of the value of $\pi$. Here we use the diagram of single-precision floats described above to extract the *sign*, *exponent*, and *fraction* of this number.

**Figure 4.7**
*Breakdown of*
`40490FDBh`

| s | exponent | fraction |
|---|----------|----------|
| 0 | 40h | 490FDBh |
| 0 | 128 | 4788187 |
| 0 | 10000000b | 100 1001 0000 1111 1101 1011b |

How can we determine what `40490FDBh` represents as a floating point number? Clearly the floating point value must be a function of these three parts. The *sign* is the quickest to dispense with.

If the sign bit is `1`, the value is negative; if the sign bit is `0`, the value is positive. The easiest way to represent this is $(-1)^{\text{Sign}}$, since $(-1)^0$ is equal to `1`, and $(-1)^1$ is equal to `-1`.

**Figure 4.8**
*Consider the Sign*

$$\texttt{Value} = (-1)^{\text{Sign}} \times \ldots$$

Next is the exponent. You might think that the value will depend on $(2)^{\text{Exponent}}$ in this case. But since we already know that the value is `3.1415927`, this dependency on the exponent cannot be correct: $2^{128}$ is greater than $3 \times 10^{38}$. But we are on the right track.

The exponent value is in fact *biased*, meaning that `127` has been added to the true exponent before storing it. Exponent values of `0` to `255` represent true 'powers of two' exponents of `-127` to `128` respectively. Therefore, the value depends not on $(2)^{\text{Exponent}}$, but in fact on $(2)^{(\text{Exponent}-127)}\ldots$

**Figure 4.9**
*Consider the Exponent*

$$\texttt{Value} = (-1)^{\text{Sign}} \times 2^{(\text{Exponent}-127)} \times \ldots$$

This leaves the last part, the *fraction*. We know that the fraction is stored as a fixed-point number. The multiplier used is $2^{23}$. Therefore, the fractional part is multiplied by $2^{23}$ when the value is stored, and is divided by $2^{23}$ when the value is extracted. Putting these three considerations together, our proposal for calculating the value as a function of the `sign`, the `exponent`, and the `fraction` is shown in Figure 4.10.

**Figure 4.10**
*Calculating the Value*

$$\texttt{Value} = (-1)^{\text{Sign}} \times 2^{(\text{Exponent}-127)} \times (\texttt{Fraction} \times 2^{-23}) \; ??$$

See if the example works:

$$\text{Value} = (-1)^{\text{Sign}} \times 2^{(\text{Exponent}-127)} \times (\text{Fraction} \times 2^{-23})$$
$$= -1^0 \times 2^{(128-127)} \times (4788187 \times 2^{-23})$$
$$= 1.1415927 \;!!$$

What happened?  This is not the value of $\pi$, at least not in this universe.

*For Ultra Techies...*

## Normalized Numbers

The problem in the preceding example is caused by a convention called *normalization*. In a *normalized* number, 1 is always added to the fractional part. This is done because if a number is expressed properly as a binary exponential number, the fractional part must be between $1.000000...b$ and $1.11111111...b$. Since the first digit must always be a 1, it is *assumed*, saving one bit of storage space. (We will talk later about *denormalized* numbers, where 1 is *not* added.) For normalized numbers, the fractional contribution to the value is $(1 + \text{Fraction} \times 2^{-23})$. Putting it all together, the expression for value is shown in Figure 4.12.

*Figure 4.12
Calculation Including
Normalization*

$$\text{Value} = (-1)^{\text{Sign}} \times 2^{(\text{Exponent}-127)} \times (1 + \text{Fraction} \times 2^{-23})$$

In this case,

*Figure 4.13
Calculation Completed*

$$\text{Value} = (-1)^{\text{Sign}} \times 2^{(\text{Exponent}-127)} \times (1 + \text{Fraction} \times 2^{-23})$$
$$= -1^0 \times 2^{(128-127)} \times (1 + 4788187 \times 2^{-23})$$
$$= 1 \times 2 \times (1 + 0.570796)$$
$$= 3.1415927$$

Success!

## VAX Floating Point

By the way, although IEEE standard floating point formats are popular, there are some very important computers that use their own formats. Perhaps the most potentially troublesome is the VAX

---

floating point standard; this is *almost* like the IEEE single-precision standard except that the VAX standard uses an exponent bias of 129 instead of 127 (!).

## Single-Precision Range of Values

You should never need to care how floating point numbers are stored. You should, however, care a *lot* about the precision and range of value of those floating point numbers. The largest positive single-precision float is $2 \times 2^{(254-127)} \approx 3.403 \times 10^{38}$.* The smallest positive number for single-precision floats is $\approx 1.175 \times 10^{-38}$.**

Many people assume that this range is good enough for everybody. Not so—consider these examples. The electron charge to the fourth power ($e^4$), a useful constant, is $5.32 \times 10^{-38}$ ESU. Some X-ray pulsars send out more than $10^{39}$ ergs of energy every second. Our galaxy contains around $10^{44}$ grams of material. But clearly, the single-precision range of values is adequate for most work.

*Astrophysicists defined: They cannot use single-precision floats because their numbers are too big.*

Note the difference between the definitions of the range of values for integers and range of values for floating point numbers. In integers, the range is defined from the smallest number to the largest number, such as from 0 to 255, or from -128 to 127. With floating point numbers we assume that numbers can be positive or negative, so instead we talk about the *absolute magnitude* of the smallest and largest numbers ($10^{-38}$ to $3 \times 10^{38}$).

## Numerical Precision of Single-Precision Floats

The numerical precision for single-precision floats is relatively limited. The result of Figure 4.12 differs from the true value of $\pi$ in the seventh place after the decimal point. But defining numerical

---

* The largest exponent value is 254 (255 is reserved for a special use), and the largest fractional value is $1.11111111.....b \approx 2$. Since all floating point numbers are *signed*, the largest negative number you can represent is $-2 \times 2^{(254-127)} \approx -3.403 \times 10^{38}$.

** The smallest exponent is 1 (0 is reserved for a special use), and the smallest fractional part is $1.0000$, so the smallest positive number is $1 \times 2^{(1-127)} \approx 1.175 \times 10^{-38}$.

---

precision is a bit more problematic for floating point numbers than it is for integers.

In integers and fixed-point numbers, the precision (smallest difference between two values) is a fixed number, such as 1 inch, $1/200$ ft., etc. This is only partially true for floating point numbers, where the smallest difference between two numbers with *the same exponent* is a fixed number. This relative difference is $2^{-23} \approx 1.1 \times 10^{-7}$. Both 3.14159265 and 3.14159264 would be stored as the same number, since they differ by only $10^{-8}$, which is less than $2^{-23} \approx 1.1 \times 10^{-7}$. The difference between the stored number and the true value of that number is called *roundoff error*.

When people talk about floating point precision, they often use the phrase *number of significant digits,* meaning the number of digits after the decimal point that they can depend on. Single-precision floating point numbers have 23 binary digits of precision (around seven digits of precision in decimal).

You are not guaranteed this precision. If you are dealing with numbers that do not have the same exponent, for example, you may get much less precision.

## Problems with Floating Point Calculations

With floating point calculations you do not have to keep track of the sign, the range of values, the multipliers, or the numerical precision. You just calculate. This ease of use is not completely free, however; there are a some subtle but major 'gotchas.'

### The Mystery of the Vanishing Significant Digits

The first problem with floating point calculations is illustrated by the exercise in Figure 4.14.

**Figure 4.14**
*Problem:*
*Vanishing Digits*

> Use your trusty scientific calculator to enter $2.490765 \times 10^{-20}$. Add to it $9.109565 \times 10^{-28}$. Subtract this result from the first number. If your calculator has lots of precision, you get $-9.11 \times 10^{-28}$. If not, you get 0.

In this exercise, you enter numbers with at least six significant digits, but when you add a small number to a large number, you can lose some or *all* of the significant digits of the smaller number! The best way to see this is to make all of the numbers have the same exponent, as shown in Figure 4.15.

**Figure 4.15**
*All Numbers with Same Exponent*

$$2.490765 \times 10^{-20} + 0.00000009109565 \times 10^{-20} = 2.4907650911 \times 10^{-20}$$

This example was produced using a calculator with twelve digits of precision, which means the last four digits of the smaller number are thrown away. In a single-precision floating point calculation, *all* of the digits of the smaller number would be thrown away.

*When evaluating the floating point accuracy of calculations, display the numbers so they all have the same exponent.*

So you are not *guaranteed* seven decimal digits of accuracy for single-precision. That is the *maximum* precision you can obtain, and then, only if all your numbers have the same exponent.

## The Case of Almost-Equal Numbers

A related 'gotcha' appears when you calculate the difference of two numbers that are very close. Figure 4.16 illustrates the problem.

**Figure 4.16**
*Problem with Almost-Equal Numbers*

An electron is being pulled by gravity $(F_{grav})$, but at the same time is being pushed by the force of radiation $(F_{rad})$. If $F_{rad} = 6.7687521 \times 10^{-15}$ and $F_{grav} = 6.7687529 \times 10^{-15}$, what is the total force $(F_{grav} - F_{rad})$ on the particle?

Using single-precision floating point calculations, that total force is zero. The unlucky electron would disagree, since it accelerates at over $10^5$ cm sec$^{-2}$[*]. But if you express the result ($8 \times 10^{-22}$) with the same exponent as the other two numbers ($0.0000008 \times 10^{-15}$), the first seven digits of the result really *are* zero!

Once again, you only get seven digits of accuracy if all numbers and *all results* are displayed with the same exponent.

---

[*] [ $(F_{grav} - F_{rad})$ divided by the electron mass ($9.1 \times 10^{-28}$ gm)]

## The Trouble with Floating Point Comparisons

One more 'gotcha' has to do with making comparisons between floating point numbers. For example, the statement

```
IF (A.EQ.B)
```

*Avoid equality checks between floating point numbers.*

is perfectly reasonable for integers. Is it reasonable for floating point numbers? If A=3.141592653 and B=3.141592652, should the program declare A equal to B, or not?

Unfortunately, different computers answer this question differently. Figure 4.17 presents an example.

**Figure 4.17**
*Problem:*
*Comparing Floating Point Numbers*

Try this code on your computer, translating, if need be, to your favorite language. Try various values for A and B.

```
REAL A,B
A = 1.00000002
B = 1.00000001
IF (((A-B).EQ.0).AND.(A.GT.B)) THEN
      WRITE (*,*) 'HI THERE'
ENDIF
```

The program checks to see if the difference between A and B is zero *and* if A is greater than B. Logically this is never true, but for some choices of A and B, and on some computers, this code segment will declare it true and print 'HI THERE' !

Non-IEEE standard arithmetic may sometimes declare that A*(B/A) is not equal to B, because the roundoff error generated by the calculation is not consistent with the roundoff error assumed by the comparison of the result with B.

The moral of this 'gotcha' is to always use computers that implement IEEE standard floating point arithmetic, which (thankfully) includes most computers produced today.

## A Bevy of Roundoff Errors

The last 'gotcha' is that roundoff error is cumulative. This problem can be especially acute for simulations that do calculations thousands or millions of times. For example, after a million calculations your roundoff error could be as large as 0.1. Even if you do not perform a million calculations, in certain cases the accumulation of error can still get you; try this exercise.

**Figure 4.18**
*Example: Roundoff Error*

> With your trusty scientific calculator, enter 2 and press the SQRT key 30 times. Next, press the $x^2$ key 30 times. My High Precision friend displays '1.98812992406'; I paid for twelve digits of precision but got one.

There is no magic solution to the accumulation of roundoff error, although using double-precision floating point numbers can help (see below). Any good book on numerical methods, such as <u>Numerical Recipes</u> (Press, Flannery, *et. al.* 1986), will give a discussion of the accumulation of error for every algorithm.

<u>Numerical Recipes</u> makes a distinction between *roundoff error*, the error introduced by the limited accuracy of the stored numbers, and what they call *truncation error*, the error introduced by the algorithm itself. For example, a routine that calculates an integral by evaluating the function value every $\Delta x$ will differ from the true value of the integral, even if all the numbers used are of infinite precision.

## The Riddle of the Stairstep Graph

> *Judy ReSyrch was interested in the differences between two of her simulations. For each simulation she calculated the vorticity as a function of distance from a fan blade. She then divided the numbers from the first simulation by the second and produced the graph shown in Figure 4.19.*

**Figure 4.19**
Single-Precision Fan Blade
Results

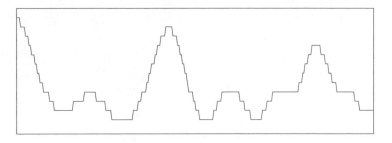

Why is the graph shaped like a stairstep? Judy was using single-precision numbers, and the ratio of the two numbers she was plotting varied from 1.0000067 to 1.0000089. The largest number differed from the smallest number only in the sixth decimal place! Therefore, there are only a few dozen unique numbers between these minimum and maximum values. The numbers that represented Judy's ratios were *discretized*, or set to one of those few unique values.

Dr. ReSyrch changed all of her variables to *double-precision* floating point numbers (see below), which uses 64 bits to define the sign, exponent, and fraction, and has approximately 14 decimal digits of numerical precision. Now the plot of the same ratio looked like this:

**Figure 4.20**
*Double-Precision Fan Blade Results*

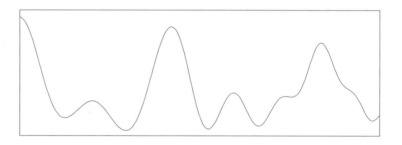

That was more like it! Dr. ReSyrch then plotted these two graphs on top of each other, as shown in Figure 4.21, to confirm their similarity.

**Figure 4.21**
*Single-Precision and Double-Precision Plots Superimposed*

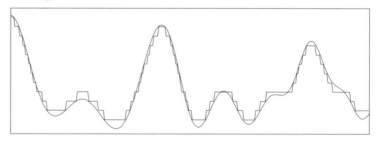

The moral of the story is…

> *Be very careful when calculating the ratio of two quite similar numbers.*

## Special Floating Point Values

Here we discuss floating point values that have special meanings in the IEEE standard formats. Not all computers use the IEEE standard, and hence they may have different special numbers. However, the general concept is the same in the various machines.

### Zero

Recall that for *normalized* numbers the first digit (1.) is assumed for the fractional part. This means that there is no way normally to represent zero. The smallest number you can represent is $\sim 10^{-38}$. So instead, the representation where both the fraction and the exponent are exactly zero is reserved to mean a true zero. To prevent a non-zero number from having this representation, the smallest allowed exponent for normalized numbers is 1.

Note that there is a nice side benefit of this choice: the bit pattern of all zeros means *zero* for bytes, integers, *and* floating point numbers!

### NaN

What is the numerical value of $\sqrt{-3.14159}$? Assuming you are not using complex numbers (see section on additional floating point formats), the result is not defined. Many computers will just bomb your program when you attempt to execute this statement. The IEEE standard does something much more useful, and sets the result to NaN, which stands for Not a Number.

A NaN is defined as a number where the exponent is 255 and the fractional part is something other than zero. To prevent valid numbers from having this representation, the largest allowed exponent for normalized numbers is 254. Figure 4.22 demonstrates the usefulness of NaN.

*Figure 4.22*
*Example of NaN*

Try this code on your computer, translating, if need be, to your favorite language:

```
REAL A
A = -81
IF (SQRT(A).EQ.9) THEN
    WRITE (*,*) 'HI THERE'
ENDIF
```

A computer without NaN support will crash on the IF statement. One with NaN support will figure out that NaN is *not* equal to 9 and skip the WRITE statement.

## INF

What is the numerical value of 1 divided by 0? As in the case of NaNs, many computers will crash when attempting this calculation. IEEE standard computers, however, will set the result to either +INF or -INF, which is short for in̲finity. Why isn't the result just set to NaN? The reason is that infinity really is a valid number. For example, 1/INF is equal to 0.

Another use of INF is to deal with *overflow*. Overflow occurs when you try to store a number that is too big for the format you are using. For example, A=B*B will generate an *overflow* condition if A and B are single-precision floats and B is equal to $10^{30}$. Non-IEEE computers may crash on overflow. IEEE computers, on the other hand, will set A to the value INF, and will let you continue calculating.

An INF is defined as a number where the exponent is 255 and the fractional part is zero. The sign defines whether the number is a +INF or a -INF. As in NaNs, normal numbers can only have exponents up to 254.

*For Ultra Techies...*

## Denormalized Numbers

Recall that for normalized numbers the fractional part is always assumed to start with a 1. In *denormalized* numbers, the fractional part is assumed to start with a 0. This is so single-precision floats can represent much smaller numbers.

For example, the smallest normalized number is $(1-2^{-23}) \times 2^{(1-127)} \approx 1.175 \times 10^{-38}$. The smallest *denormalized* number is $(0-2^{-23}) \times 2^{(1-127)} \approx 1.401 \times 10^{-45}$. By not assuming that initial 1, you can gain another seven decimal exponent digits in terms of the smallest representable number.

Once again, an exponent value of zero is used to flag that the number is denormalized. Unlike the case for the representation for zero, however, the fractional part for denormalized numbers is non-zero. And as before, normalized numbers can only have exponents down to 1.

These denormalized numbers fill in the gap, so to speak, between $-1.2 \times 10^{-38}$ and $+1.2 \times 10^{-38}$, with $2^{23}$ additional smaller values. This method reduces the problem of *underflow*, or the forcing of numbers below $10^{-38}$ to zero. Of course, numbers smaller than $1.4 \times 10^{-45}$ are set to zero even in denormalized numbers.

Figure 4.23 summarizes the contents of the sign, exponent, and fraction fields for these special floating point numbers. This table is only valid for single-precision IEEE floating point numbers.

**Figure 4.23**
*Single-Precision IEEE Floating Point Numbers*

| Name | Sign (s) | Exponent (e) | Fraction (f) | Value |
|------|----------|--------------|--------------|-------|
| Zero | 0 | 0 | 0 | 0 |
| Not a Number | any | 255 | not 0 | NaN |
| Positive Infinity | 0 | 255 | 0 | +INF |
| Negative Infinity | 1 | 255 | 0 | -INF |
| Denormalized | any | 0 | not 0 | $-1^s \times 2^{-126} \times f$ |
| Normalized | any | 1 to 254 | any | $-1^s \times 2^{(e-127)} \times (1+f)$ |

*Also For Ultra Techies...*

# Additional Floating Point Formats

Although we have only talked about the IEEE standard single-precision floating point format, there are almost as many formats as there are types of computers. But all of the format variations follow the same general outline of sign, exponent, and fraction.

We will talk about three specific formats: *double-precision floating point*, *extended-precision floating point*, and *complex numbers*.

## Double-Precision Floating Point Numbers

The format for IEEE 64-bit floating point numbers, also called double-precision float, is shown in Figure 4.24.

**Figure 4.24**
*Double-Precision Float Format*

| s | exponent | fraction |
|---|----------|----------|
| 1 | 11 bits | 52 |

The exponent has 11 bits instead of 8, the fraction 52 bits instead of 23. The exponent range for normalized doubles is $1$ to $2^{11} - 2$, or $2046$. This exponent is biased by $1023$, in the same way that the single-precision bias is $127$. Therefore, the largest normalized number is $2 \times 2^{(2046-1023)} \approx 1.798 \times 10^{308}$.

The smallest *normalized* positive number for double-precision floats is correspondingly $1 \times 2^{(1-1023)} \approx 2.225 \times 10^{-308}$. The smallest *denormalized* positive number is $2^{-52} \times 2^{(1-1023)} \approx 4.941 \times 10^{-325}$.

In Figure 4.25, we decode a double-precision number (third item listed in the quiz at the beginning of Chapter 1) the same way we previously decoded a single-precision float.

**Figure 4.25**
*Breakdown of*
400921FB54442D18h

| s | exponent | fraction |
|---|----------|----------|
| 0 | 400h | 921FB54442D18h |
| 0 | 1024 | 2,570,638,124,657,944 |
| 0 | 10000000b | 1001001000011111101101010100010001000010110100011000b |

The equation for the value of double-precision floating point numbers as a function of sign, exponent, and fraction is shown in Figure 4.26.

**Figure 4.26**
*Double-Precision Equation*

$$\text{Value} = (-1)^{\text{Sign}} \times 2^{(\text{Exponent}-1023)} \times (1 + \text{Fraction} \times 2^{-52})$$

So in this case,

**Figure 4.27**
*Example Using*
400921FB54442D18h

$$\text{Value} = (-1)^{\text{Sign}} \times 2^{(\text{Exponent}-1023)} \times (1 + \text{Fraction} \times 2^{-52})$$
$$= -1^0 \times 2^{(1024-1023)} \times (1 + 2570638124657944 \times 2^{-52})$$
$$= 1 \times 2 \times (1 + 0.570796326794897)$$
$$= 3.141592653589793$$

Note that the result is accurate to 15 decimal places. This is because the numerical precision of double-precision floating points is $2^{-52}$, or $\approx 2.22 \times 10^{-16}$. This precision yields 15 or 16 significant decimal digits. The special number formats for double-precision floats are shown in Figure 4.28.

**Figure 4.28**
*Formats for Double-Precision Floats*

| Name | Sign (s) | Exponent (e) | Fraction (f) | Value |
|------|----------|--------------|--------------|-------|
| Zero | 0 | 0 | 0 | 0 |
| Not a Number | any | 2047 | not 0 | NaN |
| Positive Infinity | 0 | 2047 | 0 | +INF |
| Negative Infinity | 1 | 2047 | 0 | -INF |
| Denormalized | any | 0 | not 0 | $-1^s \times 2^{-1022} \times f$ |
| Normalized | any | 1 to 2046 | any | $-1^s \times 2^{(e-1023)} \times (1+f)$ |

*Trivia Question:*
*If you were sending a rocket to Pluto ($5.9 \times 10^9$ km away) and your orbital calculations were perfect except that your value of $\pi$ was off in the 16th digit, by how much would your rocket miss the planet?*
*Answer: 1.3 millimeters.*

The advantages of double-precision are numerous: it is difficult to conceive a useful number outside the double-precision range of values. In addition, 15 significant digits of precision are more than enough for most calculations. Also, on many computers the speed of double-precision calculations is not much less than that for single-precision. Really, the only drawback is that double-precision numbers use twice the disk space that single-precision numbers use.

## Complex Numbers

Returning to the quiz in Chapter 1, what is the numerical value of $\sqrt{-3.14159}$? The answer is 0+1.7725**i**, where **i** is defined as $\sqrt{-1}$. (Note that disciplines such as electrical engineering use **j** to mean the same thing). Numbers that include **i** are called *complex numbers*. Complex numbers are used extensively because it is often easier to do algebra with complex than with normal numbers.

Every complex number has a *real part*, the number *without* the **i**, and an *imaginary part*, the part *with* the **i**. You might also see a complex number written as (0, 1.7725), which means exactly the same as the expression above.

To a computer, a complex number consists of two numbers: a real number and an imaginary number. In most computers the real number is stored first. Of the widely used computer languages, only FORTRAN has direct support for complex numbers.

Again in FORTRAN, complex variables can be single-precision, where real and imaginary numbers are single-precision floats, or double-precision. There are no complex integers in FORTRAN or any other language.

*If you have a legitimate calculation that needs a larger range of exponents than the extended format provides, please let me know.*

## Extended Formats

The *extended* format is even more precise than double-precision formats. These 80-bit numbers reserve 15 bits for the exponent and 63 bits for the fraction. This gives around 18 decimal significant digits and a positive data range from $10^{-4932}$ to $10^{+4932}$. Since there are $\sim 10^{80}$ particles in the known universe, the range of values for extended numbers seems large enough for any possible use. Extended numbers require more disk space and are less common and less standardized than single- and double-precision IEEE floats.

## Floating Point: Advantages & Pitfalls

For the most part, when you are using floating point calculations you do not need to think about range of values, numerical precision, or concerns with calculations. You might think of floating point as the automatic transmission of technical data storage, as it takes care of a lot of the details that you have to take care of yourself with other formats. But any new solution brings new problems...

### Computational Resources

Floating point numbers tend to take more disk space than integer or fixed-point numbers. Part of this extra space is due to extra information: every floating point number keeps track of its own exponent, whereas information on the exponent of a fixed-point number is stored outside the number. Double-precision floating point numbers, at eight bytes each, are particularly disk 'thirsty.'

### *FPUs*

The speed of calculations with floats varies widely depending on the hardware. Computers *without* floating point units (FPUs) can take a hundred times longer to do a floating point than an integer calculation. Computers *with* FPUs, which are processor chips optimized for doing floating point, may be able to do floating point calculations at virtually the same speed as integer calculations.

## *MIPS and MFLOPs*

Computers are often rated in *MIPS* and *MFLOPS*. MIPS, which stands for <u>m</u>illion <u>i</u>nstructions <u>p</u>er <u>s</u>econd, is (very) roughly proportional to the speed of integer calculations. MFLOPS, which stands for <u>m</u>illion <u>fl</u>oating <u>o</u>perations <u>p</u>er <u>s</u>econd, is a measure of the speed of floating point calculations.

If these two numbers for your computer are close, your machine is optimized for floating point. If the MIPS number for your computer is much higher than the MFLOPS number, your computer will be very slow at floating point calculations. Some MS-DOS and Macintosh computers let you decide whether to install an FPU.

## Range of Values

The range of allowed values, even for single-precision floats, is so large that most researchers have no idea of the maximum range of their numbers. Nevertheless, you should still know the range. In particular, if you deal with large items like galaxies, or small ones like nuclear cross-sections, use double-precision.

## Numerical Precision

The concept of numerical precision for floating point numbers is much more fluid than the concept of precision for integers and fixed-point numbers. The best that we can say is that the *maximum* precision for single-precision and double-precision floats is *around* 7 and 15 decimal digits, respectively.

Although the 7 digits of accuracy for single-precision may seem like a lot, if you are dealing with numbers with widely differing exponents, or numbers with a very small range, you may get into trouble. In that case, double-precision numbers are safer.

## Calculations with Floating point Numbers

Doing calculations with floating point numbers is usually an absolute dream. But do not forget those 'gotchas' described here, because when you are the most complacent they *'getcha.'*

## Portability

There are many more floating point formats than integer formats. Therefore, binary floating point files are typically not transferred between computers. Spyglass Transform has the capability of reading floating point files directly from Macintoshes, Suns, VAXes, SGIs, HPs, MS-DOS computers, and a few others.

However, floating point numbers in IEEE standard format tend to be *self-describing*, meaning that all the information about the number is stored with the number. This is contrasted with the situation with bytes, integers, and fixed-point numbers, where you must know whether the stored numbers are signed, their multipliers, etc.

*Make sure you set your file transfer program for a* binary *transfer when moving floating point files between computers, as you must do for all binary number types.*

To make your floating point numbers more portable, it is useful to consider storing your data inside an *HDF file*. HDF (Hierarchical Data Format) files can encapsulate your data and protect it from the idiosyncrasies of different computers. See Chapter 13 on the HDF file format for more information.

## Summary

Figure 4.29 compares the attributes of the different number formats discussed so far.

**Figure 4.29**
*Comparison of Different Formats*

|  | Bytes | Integers and Fixed Point | Single-Precision Floating Point | Double-Precision Floating Point |
|---|---|---|---|---|
| Computational Resources | Efficient | Efficient | Efficient* | Efficient* |
| Range of Values | Poor | Good | Excellent | Superb |
| Numerical Precision | Poor | Good | Excellent | Superb |
| Calculation Considerations | Dangerous | Be Careful | Good | Good |
| Portability | Excellent | Good | Poor | Poor |

* Depending on the hardware.

# CHAPTER 5
# ASCII TEXT NUMBERS

## ASCII Text Numbers—Introduction

Most people store their data in *ASCII text* format. In FORTRAN, it is difficult to store data in any format other than ASCII text, and ASCII text is so common some people may not be aware of any other way to store technical data.

ASCII text files are completely different from binary files (byte, integer, and floating-point). ASCII (which stands for <u>A</u>merican <u>S</u>tandard <u>C</u>ode for <u>I</u>nformation <u>I</u>nterchange) text numbers are stored as characters, in the same way that the characters in this book are stored in a disk file.

Data stored in ASCII files can be maddeningly slow to access and can occupy a great deal of disk space. However, ASCII text files are completely portable: just about any computer on the planet can read your ASCII file. More importantly, *humans* can read the file.

## ASCII Characters

English text can be represented with 26 lower-case characters, 26 upper-case characters, 10 digits, and 32 common punctuation marks (see below), for a total of 94 symbols.

**Figure 5.1**
*Common Punctuation*

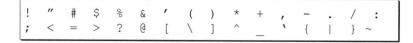

The ASCII standard is a mapping of these 94 symbols (and 34 additional *control characters*) to 128 different values, as shown in Figure 5.2. Even though you only need seven bits ($2^7=128$) to store these *ASCII characters*, by convention every character is stored in its own byte. The bottom seven bits of the byte are used to code for the character, and the top bit (the sign bit) is unused.

Some computer programs use the unused top bit for their own purposes (to flag a particular character, for example). Therefore, file transfer programs typically *mask off* this top bit, and only transmit the bottom seven bits of each byte.

**Figure 5.2**
*The 7-bit ASCII Standard*

| Decimal | Hex | Character | Comments |
|---------|-----|-----------|----------|
| 0 | 00h | NUL | Null character |
| 7 | 07h | BEL | Bell |
| 8 | 08h | BS | Backspace |
| 9 | 09h | HT | Horizontal Tab (TAB) |
| 10 | 0Ah | LF | Line Feed |
| 11 | 0Bh | VT | Vertical Tab |
| 12 | 0Ch | FF | Form Feed |
| 13 | 0Dh | CR | Carriage Return |
| 27 | 1Bh | ESC | Escape |
| 32 | 20h | SPACE | Space |
| 33—47 | 21h—2Fh | ! " # $ % & ' ( ) * + , - . / | Punctuation |
| 48—57 | 30h—39h | 0123456789 | Decimal Digits |
| 58—64 | 3Ah—3Fh | : ; < = > ? @ | Punctuation |
| 65—90 | 41h—5Ah | ABCDEFGHIJKLM NOPQRSTUVWXYZ | Capital Letters |
| 91—96 | 5Bh—60h | [ \ ] ^ _ ` | Punctuation |
| 97—122 | 61h—7Ah | abcdefghijklm nopqrstuvwxyz | Small Letters |
| 123—126 | 7Bh—7Eh | { \| } ~ | Punctuation |
| 127 | 7Fh | Del | Delete |

## Control Characters

The following control characters are used *primarily* for communications: NUL, BEL, BS, VT, ESC, and DEL. For example, BEL is supposed to beep your terminal, BS and DEL are used for telling your computer to erase the last character, and ESC is often used to tell the computer that you are beginning a special sequence. There are only five control characters in general use for storing ASCII information in files. These five characters are listed in Figure 5.3. ASCII text files usually consist of characters, punctuation, numbers, and these codes.

**Figure 5.3**
*ASCII Text File Control Codes*

| | |
|---|---|
| HT (tab) | 09h |
| LF (line feed) | 0Ah |
| FF (page eject) | 0Ch |
| CR (carriage return) | 0Dh |
| SPACE | 20h |

The ASCII standard code is used for two purposes: communicating information between computers or peripherals, and for storing information in files. Figure 5.2 does not list the characters that are used *only* for communication. These omitted characters are listed in Figure 5.4.

**Figure 5.4**
*ASCII Communication Control Characters*

```
SOH STX ETX EOT ENQ ACK SO SI DLE DC1 DC2
DC3 DC4 NAK SYN ETB CAN EM FS GS  RS  US
```

Control characters are also called *non-printing characters*, since there is no standard way to display them. In this book we will show non-printing characters with the symbol '∆'.

### Foreign Languages

ASCII is fine for English but does not include characters such as ß,ö,ü, etc. needed for other languages. Therefore, many computers use the top bit (giving an additional 128 codes) for these characters. However, there is not yet any standard for these *extended ASCII* codes. Note also that there *are* other mappings of characters to codes besides ASCII. One alternative mapping is EBCDIC. But none is as prevalent as ASCII.

### ASCII Text Strings

A group of ASCII characters strung together is known as an *ASCII text string*, or just a *text string*. For example, the ASCII characters 'P','u','f','f','i', and 'n' grouped together would represent the ASCII text string of 'Puffin.' The numerical value of this string is 50756666696Eh.

**Figure 5.5**
*The Text String* 'Puffin'

| 'P' | 'u' | 'f' | 'f' | 'i' | 'n' |
|-----|-----|-----|-----|-----|-----|
| 50h | 75h | 66h | 66h | 69h | 6Eh |
| 80 | 117 | 102 | 102 | 105 | 110 |

## ASCII Numbers

We can use ASCII text strings to write not only 'Puffin', but numbers such as '3.14159265'. Numbers coded in this way are known as ASCII text numbers, or *ASCII numbers*. Here, single quotation marks around a number indicate an ASCII text string, as opposed to a numerical value.

In binary numbers (bytes, integers, floating-point numbers), a fixed number of bytes represents a number. In contrast, an ASCII number consists of a variable number of characters, each character represented in an individual byte.

For example, let's return to the first line of the quiz in Chapter 1: '332E3134313539323635h' and decode this ASCII text number.

**Figure 5.6**
*Breakdown of*
'332E3134313539323635h'

| '3' | '.' | '1' | '4' | '1' | '5' | '9' | '2' | '6' | '5' |
|-----|-----|-----|-----|-----|-----|-----|-----|-----|-----|
| 33h | 2Eh | 31h | 34h | 31h | 35h | 39h | 32h | 36h | 35h |
| 51  | 46  | 49  | 52  | 49  | 53  | 57  | 50  | 54  | 53  |

Note that a byte can represent 256 numerical values as a binary integer, but only 10 values (0 through 9) as an ASCII text string. Apparently using ASCII text strings for storing numbers does not make very efficient use of disk space.

**Figure 5.7**
*Uses for a Byte*

| Type | Range | # of Values |
|------|-------|-------------|
| Unsigned Integer | 0 to 255 | 256 |
| Signed Integer | -128 to 127 | 256 |
| ASCII character | '0' to '9' | 10 |

What ASCII characters are needed to represent numbers?  In addition to the ASCII characters '0' through '9', you also need '.' for decimal points, and '–' for negative numbers. You may also need '+'. Finally, you need 'E' for exponential notation numbers, as described below.

## Exponential Notation ASCII Numbers

In this book we display numbers in exponential notation by superscripting the exponent ($10^{-28}$). But an ASCII text string has no way to superscript characters.

By convention ASCII text strings represent numbers in exponential notation by first displaying the fraction, followed by an 'E' (or 'e'), followed by the value of the exponent in decimal. Our example would be represented as 9.10956E-28 in this notation.

In almost all cases, a small 'e' or a capital 'E' is treated exactly the same. Note also that numbers with positive exponents, such as $1.989 \times 10^{33}$, will often be displayed as $1.989E+33$. All FORTRAN print statements precede the exponent with a '+' or '-'.

Vary rarely, you will see exponential numbers displayed in text as '9.10956*10^-28 or 9.10956*10**-28'. The '^' character means exponentiation in the BASIC language, and the '**' string means exponentiation in FORTRAN .

## Separating Numbers—ASCII Delimiters

When you store numbers in ASCII text files, you should separate each number. The problems caused by *not* doing this are illustrated by the exercise in Figure 5.8.

**Figure 5.8**
*Exercise #1*

> What numbers are represented by the string
>
> '34.562.45E+34.59-540'  ?

Several possible ways of splitting this string into numbers are listed in Figure 5.9.

**Figure 5.9**
*Possible Numbers in '34.562.45E+34.59-540'*

| | | | | | |
|------|----------|--------|------|------|------|
| 3 | 4.56 | 2.45E34 | .59 | -5 | 40 |
| 34 | .5 | 62.4 | 5e+3 | 4.59 | -540 |
| 34.56 | 2.45E+34 | .59 | -5 | 4 | 0 |

If you had stored a space character after every number, you would have generated the string shown in Figure 5.10.

**Figure 5.10**
*Different Numbers Using Spaces*

> '3  4.56  2.45E+3  4.59  -540'

It is clear what numbers *this* string represents. Here you would be using the space character as a *delimiter*, separating adjacent numbers.

## Space, Tab, and Comma as Delimiters

In addition to spaces, tabs and commas are commonly used as delimiters. Typically there will be one tab or comma between numbers, but any number of spaces between values.

| SPACE | TAB | Comma |
|-------|-----|-------|
| 20h   | 09h | 2Ch   |

ASCII text files with numbers separated by tabs are known as *Tab Delimited Files*; files with space or comma delimiters are *Space Delimited Files* or *Comma Delimited Files* (sometimes called *CSV* for Comma Separated Values).

## Storing a Position but not a Number

Sometimes people will use multiple tabs or commas between numbers to mean that a number has been skipped.

**Figure 5.12**
*Exercise #2*

> What numbers are represented by the string
>
> '3,4.56,,4.59,-540' ?

There are two ways to answer this exercise.

**Figure 5.13**
*Possible Interpretations*

| 3 | 4.56 | 4.59 | -540 |      |
|---|------|------|------|------|
| 3 | 4.56 |      | 4.59 | -540 |

For the first line in Figure 5.13 we interpret the double commas as a single separator. For the second line, we interpret the double commas as representing a position without a number. The blanks mean there is no number for that position. You must know which interpretation is intended for any specific ASCII text datafile.

Another way to represent a position that does not have a number is to store a string such as NaN or N there.

**Figure 5.14**
*Exercise #3*

> What numbers are represented by the string
>
> '3,4.56,NaN,4.59,-540' ?

The answer to this exercise is shown in the second line of Figure 5.13.

*We recommend using 'NaN' for storing a position without a number. This method is less ambiguous, and is supported by the IEEE standard.*

Sometimes people will use very large or very small numbers to represent a position without a number. For example, US Weather Survey data lists -99 for the temperature at a site that did not report the temperature at that particular time.

In any case, you must know which of these methods (if any) was used to represent a position without a number for any datafile that you read.

**Figure 5.15**
*Methods for Recording a Position without a Number*

```
Two commas
Two tabs
'NaN'
Other non-numeric characters
Out of range number (too large or small)
```

## Fixed Format Delimited Files

In a *fixed format* ASCII text file, every number starts at a particular character position and ends at a particular character position. If there is any space between numbers, it is always filled with spaces. When you read a fixed format file, you must know the starting and ending character position for every number. An example string is shown below.

**Figure 5.16**
*Sample Fixed Format File*

| Position | 1 | 2 | 3 | 4 | 5 | 6 | 7 | 8 | 9 | 10 | 11 | 12 | 13 | 14 | 15 | 16 | 17 | 18 | 19 | 20 |
|---|---|---|---|---|---|---|---|---|---|---|---|---|---|---|---|---|---|---|---|---|
| Numbers | 3 | 4 | . | 5 | 6 | 2 | . | 4 | 5 | E | + | 3 | 4 | . | 5 | 9 | - | 5 | 4 | 0 |

This string is decoded as shown in Figure 5.17.

**Figure 5.17**
Fixed Format
File Decoded

| Number Position | 1 | 2 | 3 | 4 | 5 |
|---|---|---|---|---|---|
| First Column | 1 | 2 | 6 | 13 | 17 |
| Last Column | 1 | 5 | 12 | 16 | 20 |
| Value | 3 | 4.56 | 2.45E+3 | 4.59 | -540 |

Fixed Format text is very natural in FORTRAN, where you explicitly specify the *field width* or the number of characters every number takes up. This is shown in the format statement in Figure 5.18 below.

**Figure 5.18**
*FORTRAN Format Statement for (5.12)*

```
100    FORMAT (I1,F4.2,E7.2,F4.2,I4)*
```

But fixed format datafiles are not *self-describing*, because the column 'starts' and 'ends' are not stored with the data.

You can make a fixed format file that is also space-delimited by making sure every number is delimited by at least one space, as shown in Figure 5.19.

**Figure 5.19**
*Sample Fixed Format File with Spaces*

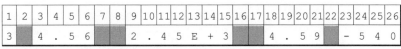

The shaded boxes represent spaces. The corresponding FORTRAN format statement is shown in Figure 5.20.

**Figure 5.20**
*FORTRAN Format Statement for (5.19)*

```
100    FORMAT (I1,1X,F4.2,2X,E7.2,2X,F4.2,1X,I4)
```

*It is a good idea to always separate your numbers with at least one space, even if it is in fixed format.*

1X represents one space, 2X represents two spaces. Instead of using 1X or 2X to insert spaces, some people separate numbers by using the format I4 to print a leading space if the number has only three digits. Don't do this! Otherwise, your numbers may or may not be separated by spaces, depending on how big your values are.

> *For example, **Dr. Wolfram Herth** wrote his groundwater data in fixed format. The first few lines from the file are shown in Figure 5.21.*

---

* I, F, and E stand for integer, float, or exponential representation. X (see Figure 5.20) stands for spaces. The numbers after I, F, and E (but before X) are the number of characters. The .2 in the F and E are the numbers after the decimal point.

---

**Figure 5.21**
*Fixed-Format*
*Groundwater Data*

```
X DISTANCE   Y DISTANCE    LEVEL
  21843.75 9086.339844 -6.821851
  21781.25 9086.339844 -6.849205
  21875.0010032.210938 -6.827897
```

He imported this dataset into his favorite Macintosh linegraphics program. That program displayed the data as shown in Figure 5.22.

**Figure 5.22**
*Groundwater Data*
*Imported into*
*Linegraphics Program*

| X Distance | Y Distance | Level |
|---|---|---|
| 21843.75 | 9086.339844 | -6.821851 |
| 21781.25 | 9086.339844 | -6.849205 |
| 21875.0010032 | .210938 | -6.827897 |

What happened?  There was no space between the X Distance and Y Distance values of the last line, so the linegraphics program did not know how to separate them. Dr. Herth then added a space after every number and tried again.

**Figure 5.23**
*Fixed-Format*
*Groundwater Data*
*with Extra Spaces*

```
X DISTANCE   Y DISTANCE    LEVEL
  21843.75   9086.339844  -6.821851
  21781.25   9086.339844  -6.849205
  21875.00  10032.210938  -6.827897
```

Now when he imported his data into his linegraphics program, he got the correct numbers, as shown in Figure 5.24.

**Figure 5.24**
*Data with Spaces, Imported*
*into Linegraphics Program*

| X Distance | Y Distance | Level |
|---|---|---|
| 21843.75 | 9086.339844 | -6.821851 |
| 21781.25 | 9086.339844 | -6.849205 |
| 21875.00 | 10032.210938 | -6.827897 |

## Delimited Files—Summary

*Tab-, space-,* and *comma-delimited files* make *no* use of the character positions of numbers, and tend to be self-describing. *Fixed format files* use character positions to define numbers, and are *not* self-describing. For example, consider the two lines of numbers shown in Figure 5.25.

**Figure 5.25**
*Two Lines*
*of Numbers*

| 3 | 4.56 | $2.45 \times 10^3$ | 4.59 | -540 |
|---|---|---|---|---|
| 7 | 8.1 | $4.302 \times 10^3$ | 12.95 | 66 |

This table of numbers is represented in Figure 5.18 as a two-line comma-delimited file. As before, shaded boxes represent spaces. Note that numbers in the same column in Figure 5.17 do not necessarily start at the same character position in Lines One and Two in Figure 5.26.

**Figure 5.26**
*Two-Line Comma-Delimited File*

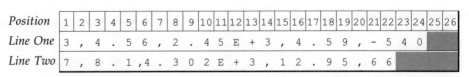

The same table is represented in Figure 5.27 as a two-line fixed-format file. Here, numbers from the same column *do* start at the same character position in Lines One and Two. Also, there is a variable number of spaces between each number, to guarantee that the numbers from the same column line up on the same positions. The file shown below could also be read as a space-delimited file, since every number is separated by at least one space.

**Figure 5.27**
*Two-Line Fixed-Format File with Spaces*

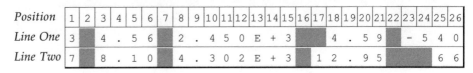

## ASCII Line Separators

We have discussed ways to delimit, or separate, numbers in lines of ASCII text. How can you separate each *line*? The unfortunate answer is that it depends on the computer you are using.

UNIX computers always use LF (0Ah) to separate lines of text. The Macintosh uses CR (0Dh). MS-DOS and VMS computers use CR *followed by* LF to separate lines.

**Figure 5.28**
*Line Separators by Computer*

| Computer | Line Separator | Hex |
|----------|----------------|-----|
| Macintosh | CR | 0Dh |
| UNIX | LF | 0Ah |
| MS-DOS | CR, LF | 0D0Ah |
| VAX VMS | CR, LF | 0D0Ah |

Originally CR meant a return to column one (no line advance) and LF meant line advance (no return to column one). The MS-DOS/VMS convention is consistent with this original meaning. But although having separate control characters for CR and LF makes sense for printers, it makes no sense for datafiles.

For ASCII text files all that is needed is a *line separator*, hence UNIX and Macintosh use just one of the two characters to represent it. Unfortunately, these computers use different characters, so if you write an ASCII text file on one type of computer and read it on another, chances are you will not get what you want.

Figure 5.17 shows what you will see in a text editor on the 'Read' computer, after writing

```
HI
BYE
```

in a file on the 'Write' computer and then transferring it. The 'Δ' symbol stands for non-printing characters such as CR or LF.

**Figure 5.29**
*Reading and Writing*
'HI
BYE'

| | Read on Macintosh | Read on UNIX | Read on VMS/MSDOS |
|---|---|---|---|
| *Write on Macintosh* | HI<br>BYE | HIΔBYE | HIΔBYE |
| *Write on UNIX* | HIΔBYE | HI<br>BYE | HIΔBYE |
| *Write on VMS/MSDOS* | HI<br>ΔBYE | HIΔ<br>BYE | HI<br>BYE |

You might be using a mixture of computers now and never have this problem, because the default mode of text in the transfer programs FTP, KERMIT, or XMODEM converts the line separators for you.

**Figure 5.30**
*Exercise #4*

Transfer an ASCII Text file between dissimilar computers using both binary and text file transfers. Compare the two files in a text editor.

## Binary vs. ASCII Text File Transfers

A `binary` file transfer does not change the datafile in any way. Any binary format file (byte, integer, floating point), or binary file format *standard* such as HDF, must be transferred using binary.

A `text` (or `ASCII`) file transfer does two things: first it (usually) strips off the top bit of every byte; second, it changes the line separators to whatever is appropriate for the reading computer. Both of these actions are absolutely *deadly* for binary files.

For example, if you wrote a byte file on a UNIX computer and then moved it to a Macintosh using a `text` file transfer, all bytes equal to 10 (0Ah) would be changed to 13 (0Dh).

*Figure 5.31*
*Exercise #5*

> Transfer a binary byte file between dissimilar computers using both binary and text file mode. Compare the two files.

*ASCII text files consist of ASCII characters only. Anything else is a binary file.*

Sometimes it might not be clear what is a binary and what is a text file. For example, the disk file that holds the contents of this book consists primarily of *text*. However, it is in fact a *binary* file, at least for the purposes of file transfer. That is because the program used to write the file (Microsoft Word) includes much more than just ASCII characters, such as formatting information, etc.

*For Real Techies...*

### NFS Mounts

If you use `text` or `binary` appropriately on your file transfers, you may never need to know the details of line separators and file conversions, *unless you use NFS (Network File System) software between dissimilar computers.*

NFS software lets you treat a disk drive on a remote computer as if it were physically on your computer. The problem is that NFS has no absolute way to know whether a particular file is a binary or ASCII text file.

If NFS does *no* conversions, your binary files are safe, but your ASCII text files may not be editable. For example, if you read a text file on a UNIX disk drive using a Macintosh program, the entire file will look like it is one line (the UNIX LF is treated as a non-printing character and not as a line separator).

Because of this, a few NFS implementations try to figure out whether a file is binary or ASCII text. This is done by looking at the file name, the file contents, or the file type (in the case of the Macintosh).

This works most of the time, *but not all of the time*. Sometimes, your text files will not get converted. What is worse is when your *binary* files *do* get converted.

In any case, be aware (and beware).

## ASCII Text: Advantages & Pitfalls

### Computational Resources

An ASCII text datafile can take two to five times the disk space of a comparable binary datafile. Not only is there less information in each byte in an ASCII file (10 values per byte instead of 256), but extra bytes are needed for decimal points, exponents, delimiters, and line separators.

Computers cannot do calculations with ASCII numbers. Therefore, your data must be converted *from* binary numbers when storing ASCII text datafiles and must be converted *to* binary numbers when reading ASCII text files. This conversion process is computationally expensive.

*What the world needs is a file format with the efficiency of a binary format but the portability and the self-describing capability of an ASCII text format.*
*It's here—*
*see Chapter 13.*

Not only that, but there is no way to *randomly access* a number in an ASCII text datafile. This is because in a binary file every number takes a fixed number of bytes, but in an ASCII text file each number takes a variable number of bytes.

Therefore, in a binary file you can read the 7,000th number without having to read the previous 6,999 values. But in an ASCII datafile, you must *sequentially read* the leading 6,999 values before getting to the one you want.

The saving grace of ASCII text files is that they can be read by humans and can be self-describing, in that the format and what the data means are in the datafile itself.

## Range of Values

Unlike binary numbers, ASCII numbers do not have a fixed size. Therefore, the concept of 'range of values' does not mean much for ASCII numbers. If you need to express very large or very small numbers, you just use more numbers for the exponent.

You can, however, run into problems trying to read these numbers. Computers convert ASCII numbers into binary numbers as they are read, so you must make sure the binary number format you read *into* can handle the size of the original ASCII number.

## Numerical Precision

Since ASCII numbers do not have a fixed size, your numerical precision varies with the number of digits you use. Note also that '3.14159' is stored as exactly that, and not as '3.141599999' (as might be the case with single-precision floats).

You must be careful when reading ASCII text files. You can store '3.141592653589793' as an ASCII number, but if you read it in with a single-precision float you will lose most of that numerical precision.

## Calculations with ASCII Text

You cannot do calculations with ASCII text. You must convert the text numbers to binary numbers first. Be sure to use a binary format with sufficient range of values and numerical precision for your data.

## Portability

ASCII text datafiles are the most portable datafiles, as long as the difference in line separators is taken care of. Figure 5.32 lists rules of conduct for creating ASCII text datafiles.

**Figure 5.32**
*Rules for Creating ASCII
Text Datafiles*

**Rule 1:** Make your ASCII text file self-describing.
You can do this by listing the file format and
the meaning of the data in text in the
beginning of the file.

**Rule 2:** Always leave spaces between every number
pair, even if you are writing a fixed-format
file. This makes the data more human-
readable.

**Rule 3:** Use NaN to record a position without a
number.

Figures 5.33 and 5.34 are ASCII text file examples that represent
the same data. Which file format would you rather read?

**Figure 5.33**
*A Bad Example of
an ASCII Text File*

```
4158095.30 2769728.30 15.00  5.00 1020.60 -0.31 2.55
4206175.00 2711076.00 17.00  5.00 1022.30 -0.52 4.09
4157729.80 2479427.00 24.00  7.00 1025.70 -1.21 4.47
3925337.00 2395113.80 27.00 11.00 1026.70 -1.06 5.04
3975751.30 2386686.80 22.00  7.00 1025.40 -0.89 4.02
4015575.80 2339392.30 -99.00 -99.00 1027.40 2.50 3.28
4151424.80 2401246.50 25.00 10.00 1026.70 0.68 2.48
4089275.00 2322289.50 27.00  4.00 1027.10 2.24 2.13
4105378.00 2298648.30 30.00 14.00 1027.80 3.60 0.22
4102765.80 2221281.00 25.00  4.00 1026.40 4.26 1.82
4157063.30 2257515.30 32.00  8.00 1029.10 3.03 4.16
```

The datafile in Figure 5.33 is a space-delimited file. You must know
what each column means, and that '-99.00' means 'no data'.

*Figure 5.34*
*Good Example of*
*an ASCII Text File*

```
#Data recorded 01/02/91 at 694 stations. NaN means no data.
# X and Y is Lat-Long mapped onto polar stereographic projection
# X-coord    Y-coord    Temp(F) Dewpt(F) Press(Mb) U(m/s) V(m/s)
4158095.30  2769728.30  15.00    5.00    1020.60  -0.31  2.55
4206175.00  2711076.00  17.00    5.00    1022.30  -0.52  4.09
4157729.80  2479427.00  24.00    7.00    1025.70  -1.21  4.47
3925337.00  2395113.80  27.00   11.00    1026.70  -1.06  5.04
3975751.30  2386686.80  22.00    7.00    1025.40  -0.89  4.02
4015575.80  2339392.30  NaN      NaN     1027.40   2.5   3.28
4151424.80  2401246.50  25.00   10.00    1026.70   0.68  2.48
4089275.00  2322289.50  27.00    4.00    1027.10   2.24  2.13
4105378.00  2298648.30  30.00   14.00    1027.80   3.60  0.22
4102765.80  2221281.00  25.00    4.00    1026.40   4.26  1.82
4157063.30  2257515.30  32.00    8.00    1029.10   3.03  4.16
```

The datafile in Figure 5.34 is a fixed format file, with spaces separating all numbers. NaN is used for positions without a number, and the first three lines of the file are descriptive. This file is human *and* computer readable.

## Summary

*Figure 5.35*
*Summary of*
*Number Types*

Figure 5.35 compares the different number formats we have discussed in the first five chapters.

|  | Bytes | Integers and Fixed-Point | Single-Precision Floating Point | Double-Precision Floating Point | ASCII Text |
|---|---|---|---|---|---|
| Computational Resources | Efficient | Efficient | Efficient* | Efficient* | Very Slow |
| Range of Values | Poor | Good | Excellent | Superb | Variable |
| Numerical Precision | Poor | Good | Excellent | Superb | Variable |
| Calculation Considerations | Dangerous | Be Careful | Good | Good | Not Possible |
| Portability | Excellent | Good | Poor | Poor | Superb |

* Depending on the hardware

# PART III
# THE DATA UNIVERSE

*How many dimensions does your data have?*

*How is your data organized on disk?*

*Have you considered changing the dimensionality of your data to help you graph and analyze it?*

*What are your independent variables, and what are your dependent variables?*

If you have had problems answering these questions for your data, you should read the next few chapters. Chapter 6 discusses data *dimensionality* and *organization*, and gives you a road map of the data universe. Chapters 7 through 10 describe each of these datafile types in much greater detail. Chapter 11 lists the techniques for converting from one data organization to another, and for adding dimensions to your data.

# CHAPTER 6
# A MAP OF THE
# DATA UNIVERSE

## OVERVIEW

In this chapter we discuss data *dimensionality* and *organization*, We show that data can be organized as *column* datafiles, *2D matrix* datafiles, *3D matrix* datafiles, and *polygonal* datafiles.

## Data Values, Locations, and Descriptions

Raw numbers are meaningless without some sort of context. For example, consider the following exercise.

*Exercise: what do the following numbers mean?*

```
-3.2,-12.3,10.1,21.6,53.1,56,
62.1,55.1,41.4,26.4,-1.0,5.4
```

It is impossible to give an answer to the exercise without knowing more. Telling you that the numbers are measurements recorded in 1955 in Fairbanks, Alaska helps, but something is still missing.

What is missing is another set of numbers that you can relate to this data. We call this new set of numbers the *data locations* for the *data value*.

*Exercise: what do the numbers in Figure 6.1 mean?*

**Figure 6.1**
*Table of Average Temperatures (1955) in Fairbanks, Alaska*

| Month Name | Month Number | Temperature (F) |
|---|---|---|
| January | 1 | -3.2 |
| February | 2 | -12.3 |
| March | 3 | 10.1 |
| April | 4 | 21.6 |
| May | 5 | 53.1 |
| June | 6 | 56.0 |
| July | 7 | 62.1 |
| August | 8 | 55.1 |
| September | 9 | 41.4 |
| October | 10 | 26.4 |
| November | 11 | -1.0 |
| December | 12 | 5.4 |

Now every *data value* (temperature) has a *data location* (month number) associated with it. (The datafile contains another column, Month Name, which we are disregarding for now.) Once each data value has a data location, we can make a linegraph of the data, as shown in Figure 6.2.

**Figure 6.2**
*Graph of Average Temperatures (1955) in Fairbanks, Alaska*

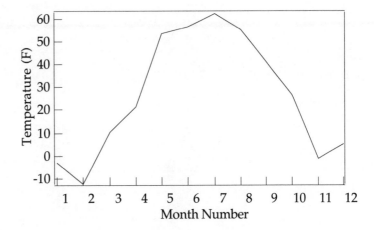

## Defining Data Location

We define data locations as the information needed to give a particular data value *organization and location*. In the example above, the month is the data location for the data value of temperature. The map coordinates of the measurements (Fairbanks, Alaska) are *not* data locations, because they are the same for all data values in the dataset. Instead, they are part of the *description* of the dataset. With these definitions we can categorize the datafile first presented in Figure 6.1 as shown below.

**Figure 6.3**
*Data, Location, and Description for Dataset Shown in Figure 6.1*

| Data Value | Temperature (degrees F) |
|---|---|
| Data Location | Month Number |
| Data Description | Fairbanks, Alaska, 1955 |

## Independent Variables and Dependent Variables

When plotting a function such as $y=\sin(x)$, one often hears $x$ called the *independent variable* (for the parameter that you can *vary independently*), and $y$ the *dependent variable* (for the parameter that *depends* on the independent variable). These concepts for the graphing of functions are completely analogous to our terms of data location and value for the graphing of data, as shown in Figure 6.4.

*Figure 6.4*
*Definitions of Data,*
*Data Location, and*
*Data Description*

| Data Values | Dependent Variables | The values you are interested in. |
|---|---|---|
| Data Locations | Independent Variables | Numbers unique to every data value that organize and locate the data. |
| Data Description | | Numbers or words that are relevant for all values in the dataset. |

## US Weather Example

A more detailed example is shown in Figure 6.5, which shows the first few lines of a datafile of weather measurements taken across the United States on a particular day.

*Exercise: Identify the data values, locations, and description for the dataset shown in Figure 6.5.*

*Figure 6.5*
*US Weather*
*Measurements*
*on Jan. 2, 1991.*

```
#Data recorded 01/02/91 at 694 stations. NaN means no data.
# X and Y is Lat-Long mapped onto polar stereographic projection
# X-coord    Y-coord    Temp(F)  Dewpt(F)  Press(Mb)  U(m/s)  V(m/s)
4158095.30  2769728.30  15.00    5.00      1020.60    -0.31   2.55
4206175.00  2711076.00  17.00    5.00      1022.30    -0.52   4.09
4157729.80  2479427.00  24.00    7.00      1025.70    -1.21   4.47
3925337.00  2395113.80  27.00    11.00     1026.70    -1.06   5.04
3975751.30  2386686.80  22.00    7.00      1025.40    -0.89   4.02
4015575.80  2339392.30  NaN      NaN       1027.40    2.5     3.28
    •           •          •        •          •         •       •
```

One way to organize this datafile is shown in Figure 6.6.

**Figure 6.6**
*Data, Location, and
Description for Datafile
Shown in Figure 6.5*

| Data Values | Temperature   (degrees F)<br>Dew Point   (degrees F)<br>Pressure (milliBars)<br>East-West Wind (meters/sec)<br>North-South Wind (meters/sec) |
|---|---|
| Data Locations | X-Map Coordinate<br>Y-Map Coordinate |
| Data Description | United States measurements<br>taken on January 2, 1991 |

Every data location pair has *five* data values (Temperature, Dew Point, etc.), and every data value has *two* data locations (X-Map, Y-Map Coordinates). The basic idea remains the same here as in Figure 6.1: every value has associated with it a set of locations.

## The Dimensionality of Data

The number of location values associated with every data value defines the *dimensionality* of the dataset. Figure 6.1 consists of a single *1-dimensional* dataset, since there is only one data location per data value.

**Dimensionality**
*The number of data locations.*

The datafile in Figure 6.5 consists of *five 2-dimensional* datasets. The datasets are 2-dimensional because there are two data locations (X-Map coordinates, Y-Map coordinates) for every data value. There are five datasets because for each data location pair there are five data values (Temperature, Dew Point, Pressure, E-W Wind, N-S Wind).

Figure 6.7 is a 2-dimensional scatter plot of one of these datasets. We used the data locations (X-Map, Y-Map Coordinates) to position dots on the graph, and the data value (Temperature) to color the dots. Here light dots represent low temperatures, and dark dots represent high temperatures.[*]

---

[*] All grayscale images in this book were generated using Spyglass Transform, and annotated using Spyglass Format.

**Figure 6.7**
*Scatter Plot of*
*Temperature Measurements*
*from Figure 6.5*

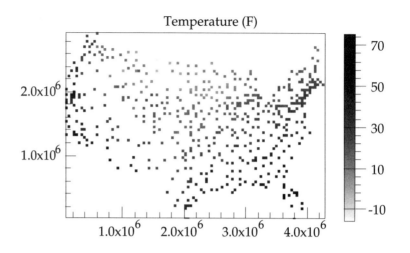

## Adding a Dimension

In Figure 6.8 we show a datafile similar to the one shown in Figure 6.5, except that a new column of `Altitude` has been added.

**Figure 6.8**
*US Weather Measurements*
*with Altitude on Jan. 2, 1991*

```
#Temp recorded at various stations and
altitudes
# X-coord     Y-coord       Alt (ft)   Temp(F)
4158095.30   2769728.30      1231.2     45.30
4206175.00   2711076.00       932.1     38.50
4157729.80   2479427.00      7843.9     11.27
3925337.00   2395113.80      3489.2     19.64
3975751.30   2386686.80        75.4     52.00
4015575.80   2339392.30        NaN       NaN
     •            •             •         •
```

One way to categorize this new dataset is shown in Figure 6.9.

**Figure 6.9**
*Data, Location, and*
*Description for Datafile*
*Shown in Figure 6.8*

| Data Values | Temperature    (degrees F)<br>Altitude (feet) |
|---|---|
| Data Locations | X-Map Coordinate<br>Y-Map Coordinate |
| Data Description | Measurements with altitude<br>taken across the United States |

Data organized this way is still 2-dimensional, since there are two data locations for each data value. However, to display all the data you would need *two* 2-dimensional datasets. The plot of either of these datasets would be similar to that shown in Figure 6.7.

You can also organize the datafile as a 3-dimensional dataset, shown in Figure 6.10.

**Figure 6.10**
*Alternate Data, Location, and Description for Datafile Shown in Figure 6.8*

| Data Value | Temperature   (degrees F) |
|---|---|
| Data Locations | X-Map Coordinate<br>Y-Map Coordinate<br>Altitude (feet) |
| Data Description | Measurements with altitude taken across the United States |

`Altitude`, which was previously considered a data value, has been redefined as a third data *location*. Now we have three data locations for each data value, making this a 3-dimensional dataset. This dataset could be plotted as a 3-dimensional scatter plot, as you will see in Chapter 7.

*Always know your data values, locations, and dimensionality.*

These examples show that the dimensionality of a datafile is not fixed; you can manipulate the dimensionality to maximize insight into the data. We will show several examples of changing dimensionality in the chapters that follow.

You must at all times, however, be aware of your choices for data values, locations, and dimensionality.

## Organizing Data Storage

The examples given above were stored on the computer as *column* data. There are other ways to organize data, such as 2D *matrix* data, *3D matrix* data, and *polygonal* data.

We will touch briefly on each group here. The remaining chapters in Part III are devoted to in-depth explorations of each of these data organization groups.

### Column Data

Column datafiles consist of a series of named columns, some for values and some for locations. Column datafiles are typically ASCII text files, with spaces or tabs between the column entries and line separators (CR, LF) between the rows. Items in a particular row are considered a single *record*. Items in a column may be numbers, or they may be text strings, as in Figures 6.1, 6.5, and 6.8.

Another example of a column datafile is shown in Figure 6.11. There are two data *location* columns (X, Y) and one data *value* column (Velocity). This datafile therefore comprises a single *2-dimensional* dataset.

**Figure 6.11**
*Column Data Example*

| X | Y | Velocity |
|---|---|----------|
| 0.5 | 0.5 | 0.0350 |
| 0.5 | 1.0 | 0.0714 |
| 0.5 | 1.5 | 0.3853 |
| 1.0 | 0.5 | 0.4911 |
| 1.0 | 1.0 | 0.2422 |
| 1.0 | 1.5 | 0.9207 |
| 1.5 | 0.5 | 0.5744 |
| 1.5 | 1.0 | 0.3305 |
| 1.5 | 1.5 | 0.8485 |

We talk more about column datafiles in Chapter 7.

## 2D Matrix Data

A plot of the X, Y coordinates of Figure 6.11 on a scatter plot (ignoring Velocity for the moment) shows that the locations fall on a regular grid.

**Figure 6.12**
*Scatter Plot for Figure 6.11*

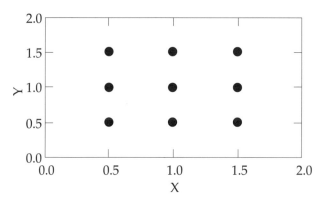

Can we make use of this regularity to save disk space? The answer is yes, since we clearly do not need to store the X, Y coordinates for every data value for this dataset. We can store this file more efficiently as a *2-dimensional (2D) matrix*.

|   |     | X | | |
|---|-----|--------|--------|--------|
|   |     | **0.5** | **1.0** | **1.5** |
|     | **0.5** | 0.0350 | 0.4911 | 0.5744 |
| **Y** | **1.0** | 0.0714 | 0.2422 | 0.3305 |
|     | **1.5** | 0.3853 | 0.9207 | 0.8485 |

In Figure 6.13, the X, Y coordinates for a particular data value are given implicitly by the position of that data value in the matrix. This saves having to repeat X, Y coordinates. We talk more about 2D matrix files in Chapter 8.

## 3D Matrix Data

We can easily extend the idea of 2D matrix datafiles to 3D matrix datafiles. Consider Figure 6.11, which shows selected parts of a 3-dimensional column dataset. The original data has $3 \times 3 \times 3 = 27$ entries, for the three values of X, three values of Y, and three values of Z.

*Figure 6.14*
*3D Column Data Example*

| X | Y | Z | Velocity |
|-----|-----|-----|----------|
| 0.5 | 0.5 | 0.0 | 0.0350 |
| 0.5 | 1.0 | 0.0 | 0.0714 |
| 0.5 | 1.5 | 0.0 | 0.3853 |
| 1.0 | 0.5 | 0.0 | 0.4911 |
| 1.0 | 1.0 | 0.0 | 0.2422 |
| 1.0 | 1.5 | 0.0 | 0.9207 |
| 1.5 | 0.5 | 0.0 | 1.6070 |
| 1.5 | 1.0 | 0.0 | 1.1980 |
| 1.5 | 1.5 | 0.0 | 0.8690 |
| 0.5 | 0.5 | 3.0 | 0.6250 |
| 0.5 | 1.0 | 3.0 | 0.4754 |
| 0.5 | 1.5 | 3.0 | 0.4043 |
| 1.0 | 0.5 | 3.0 | 0.3673 |
| 1.0 | 1.0 | 3.0 | 0.3096 |
| 1.0 | 1.5 | 3.0 | 0.1824 |
| 1.5 | 0.5 | 3.0 | 1.7672 |
| 1.5 | 1.0 | 3.0 | 1.7253 |
| 1.5 | 1.5 | 3.0 | 1.7757 |
| 0.5 | 0.5 | 6.0 | 1.1853 |
| 0.5 | 1.0 | 6.0 | 0.9144 |
| 0.5 | 1.5 | 6.0 | 0.7263 |
| 1.0 | 0.5 | 6.0 | 0.6164 |
| 1.0 | 1.0 | 6.0 | 0.5557 |
| 1.0 | 1.5 | 6.0 | 0.4966 |
| 1.5 | 0.5 | 6.0 | 2.4064 |
| 1.5 | 1.0 | 6.0 | 2.5157 |
| 1.5 | 1.5 | 6.0 | 2.7190 |

It is natural to select X, Y, and Z as the data locations and Velocity as the data value, giving us a single 3-dimensional dataset. Since the data falls on a uniform $3 \times 3 \times 3$ grid, it is natural to consider storing the data as a 3D matrix, in the same way that we stored data on a $3 \times 3$ grid as a 2D matrix.

In Figure 6.15 we show the data from Figure 6.14 in 3D matrix format.

**Figure 6.15**
*Data from Figure 6.14 Stored as a 3D Matrix File*

| | Z=6.0 | 0.5 | 1.0 | 1.5 | |
|---|---|---|---|---|---|
| | Z=3.0 | 0.5 | 1.0 | 1.5 | 2.4064 |
| Z=0.0 | 0.5 | 1.0 | 1.5 | 1.7672 | 2.5157 |
| 0.5 | 0.0350 | 0.4911 | 0.5744 | 1.7253 | 2.7190 |
| 1.0 | 0.0714 | 0.2422 | 0.3305 | 1.7757 | |
| 1.5 | 0.3853 | 0.9207 | 0.8485 | | |

The 3D matrix is shown as a series of 2D matrix layers. The top layer is labeled Z=0.0; the Z=3.0 and Z=6.0 layers are partially obscured.

For the dataset in Figure 6.14 we need $27 \times 3 = 81$ numbers to store all of the data values. Storing the same information as a 3D matrix file requires only $27+3+3+3=36$ numbers. We talk more about 3D matrix files in Chapter 9.

## Polygonal Data

Polygonal information is actually stored as a column datafile. There are some special features of polygonal datafiles, which is why we talk about them separately.

A polygonal datafile consists of a list of polygons. Stored with each polygon is information such as the location of the polygon, the locations of the polygonal vertices, and any physical values such as temperature, stress, etc. An example of a polygonal datafile is shown below.

**Figure 6.16**
*A Sample Polygon File*

| Polygon Name | Polygon Position | Vertices | Temp. | Stress |
|---|---|---|---|---|
| A | (0.5,0.5,0.0) | (vertex info) | 72.2 | 0.034 |
| B | (0.5,1.0,0.5) | • | 74.8 | 0.056 |
| C | (1.0,0.5,0.5) | • | 71.3 | 0.089 |
| • | • | • | • | • |

This sample dataset is a record of a model of a cube, with information on each facet of the cube.

**Figure 6.17**
*Cube Model for Data
in Figure 6.13*

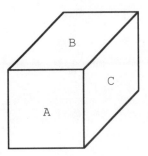

We talk more about polygonal datafiles in Chapter 10.

## Summary

This chapter has introduced the concepts of datafile, dataset, data dimensionality, independent and dependent variables, data location, data value, and data description. You saw that column data can sometimes be stored more efficiently as 2D or 3D matrix data. A brief example showed that one sample datafile could be organized as either two 2D datasets, or one 3D dataset. These topics will be further expanded in the remaining chapters in this section.

# CHAPTER 7
# COLUMN DATA

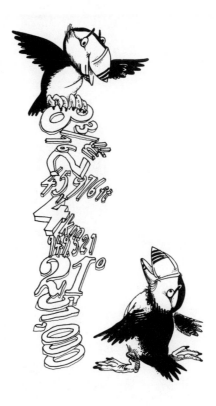

# OVERVIEW

The most common way to organize data on disk is as a *column*
datafile. Most column datafiles are ASCII text files. In this
chapter we discuss how column data is stored on disk and the most
common ways of visualizing column datasets. In particular, we
show how you can change the dimensionality of column dataset for
better analysis and visualization.

## Column Datafiles on Disk

Column data can be stored as binary numbers, typically using a
standard data format such as HDF (see Chapter 13). However, in
the overwhelming majority of cases, column data is stored as ASCII
text numbers. As an example, the first few lines of an ASCII text
column datafile are given below.

*Figure 7.1*
*US Weather*
*on Jan. 2, 1991*

```
#Data on 01/02/91 at 694 stations. NaN = no data.
#X and Y is Lat-Long in polar stereographic proj.
# X-coord   Y-coord   Temp(F) Dewpt(F) Press(Mb)
4158095.3  2769728.3  15.00   5.00     1020.60
4206175.0  2711076.0  17.00   5.00     1022.30
4157729.8  2479427.0  24.00   7.00     1025.70
4015575.8  2339392.3  NaN     NaN      1027.40
     .          .        .      .          .
```

The first two lines of Figure 7.1 are *header lines*. These are lines of
text that precede the data and typically include a description of
the data. The next line is the *title line*, which displays a title for
every column in the datafile.

The rest of the datafile holds the actual data values. In this
example, every data line consists of five entries, one for every
column. The entries are separated here by spaces, although they
could also be separated by other delimiters such as tabs or commas.
Every line ends in the line separator appropriate for the computer
used to generate the file.

**Figure 7.2**
*Breakdown of*
*Figure 7.1 Datafile*

| Header Line | #Data on 01/02/91 at 694 stations. NaN = no data. | | | | |
|---|---|---|---|---|---|
| Header Line | #X and Y is Lat-Long in polar sterographic proj. | | | | |
| Title Line | X-coord | Y-coord | Temp(F) | Dewpt(F) | Press(Mb) |
| Data | 4158095.3 | 2769728.3 | 15.00 | 5.00 | 1020.60 |
| | 4206175.0 | 2711076.0 | 17.00 | 5.00 | 1022.30 |
| | 4157729.8 | 2479427.0 | 24.00 | 7.00 | 1025.70 |
| | 4015575.8 | 2339392.3 | NaN | NaN | 1027.40 |
| | • | • | • | • | • |

*Self describing column datafiles have header lines and title lines.*

Although not all ASCII column datafiles have header lines and title lines, they *should*. Having headers and titles makes the datafile *self describing*—the datafile includes all the information needed to analyze the data it contains.

## Text String Columns

Data columns do not have to be numeric: they can consist of ASCII text strings. However, you must be use delimiters carefully when you have text columns. Consider the following ASCII text example.

**Figure 7.3**
*Column Datafile*
*with Text Columns*

```
Pizza Money from Employees at Spyglass, Inc.
Name            Employee_ID      Age     Donation
John Smith           2343         23     $00.23
Barbra A. Jones      9434         12     $04.10
James Brown          0032         86     $-0.56
Madonna              0000         51     $97.00
```

We would be asking for trouble if we were to use *spaces* as delimiters in the datafile shown in Figure 7.3. The datafile would be read as shown in the figure below.

**Figure 7.4**
*Breakdown of*
*Figure 7.3 Dataset*

| Header Line | Pizza Money from Employees at Spyglass, Inc. | | | | |
|---|---|---|---|---|---|
| Title Line | Name | Employee ID | Age | Donation | |
| Data | John | Smith | 2343 | 23 | $00.23 |
| | Barbra | A. | Jones | 9434 | 12 | $04.10 |
| | James | Brown | 0032 | 86 | $-0.56 |
| | Madonna | 0000 | 51 | $97.00 | |

*Never include the delimiter character in a text string.*

This is not the breakdown we wanted. The problem is that every space has been interpreted as a column delimiter, including those spaces that are part of names. For this datafile the best delimiters would be commas or tabs.

## Visualizing Column Data

As discussed in Chapter 6, column datafiles can contain 1D datasets, 2D datasets, 3D datasets, even N-dimensional datasets. Each dimensionality has associated with it common visualization techniques, described below.

### Linegraphs and Bar Charts

The most common way to graph 1-dimensional column data is with *linegraphs* or with *bar charts*. In a linegraph, each pair (data value-data location) is plotted on an X-Y graph. Symbols may or may not be placed at these points. Finally, the points are connected by lines, drawn in order of increasing X location. Shown below is a linegraph example repeated from Chapter 6.

**Figure 7.5**
*Linegraph of Average Temperatures (1955) in Fairbanks, Alaska*

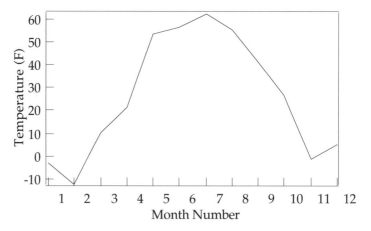

Plotting multiple 1-dimensional datasets on the same graph is usually a simple matter, though it is important to differentiate the lines representing the datasets. There are many techniques for doing this. Possibly the simplest is the technique used in this book: placing a text label directly over each line (see Figure 7.12).

Another common way to graph 1-dimensional data is the bar chart, where each value-location pair is plotted as the top value in a bar extending from the Y-axis to that point. Figure 7.6 is a bar chart of the data that was used to plot Figure 7.5.

**Figure 7.6**
*Bar Chart of Average Temperatures (1955) in Fairbanks, Alaska*

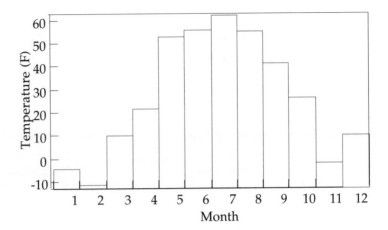

Visualizing large amounts of technical data using bar charts is problematic for the following reasons:

> *Bar charts cannot be used when the spacing of the data locations is uneven because the bars would be unevenly spaced.*
>
> *It is difficult to plot multiple 1-dimensional datasets on the same graph using bar charts.*
>
> *On commonly available paper, bar charts cannot be used to plot more than about 100 datapoints, because the bars become so narrow they approximate lines.*

## Scatter Plots and Parametric Plots

Linegraphs and bar charts are for plotting 1-dimensional datasets. The location variable corresponds to the X-axis, and the data value corresponds to the Y-axis. The value (Y-axis) is graphed as a function of the location (X-axis).

*Scatter plots* are for plotting 2-dimensional or 3-dimensional datasets. With these, *both* the X-axis *and* the Y-axis (and the Z-axis in the case of 3D) correspond to the location values. A representation of the data value is then plotted at that location.

**Linegraphs** *are for plotting multiple 1D datasets.*
**Scatter** *plots are for plotting a single 2D or 3D dataset.*

For example, in this plot repeated from Chapter 6, the data value of `Temperature` is represented as the intensity of a dot at each location.

**Figure 7.7**
*Scatter Plot of US Temperature Measurements*

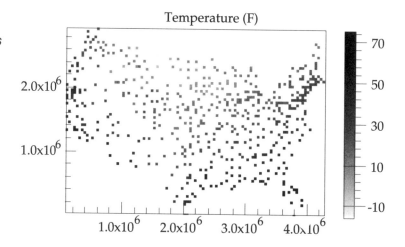

Temperature (F)

## Parametric Plots vs. Linegraphs

A *parametric plot* is a scatter plot with lines drawn between the plotted values. Parametric plots are commonly confused with linegraphs, but there are fundamental differences.

A linegraph is the data equivalent of plotting a function like `y=sin(x)`. There can only be one y value (data value) for every x value (data location). In a linegraph, the order of data values and locations does not matter, because lines are drawn between the value-location pairs in order of increasing data location.

A parametric plot is the data equivalent of plotting a function like `(x=sin(t),y=sin(t/3))`, where t varies from a certain range. There can be multiple y values (data values) for every x value (data location). In most cases, the path that the parametric plot takes is governed by the order of the data values and locations in the columns.

**Figure 7.8**
*Linegraphs vs.*
*Parametric Plots*

| Linegraphs | Parametric Plots |
|---|---|
| y=sin(x) | x=sin(t), y=sin(t/3) |
| Single y values | Multiple y values |
| Data order does not matter | Data order matters |

An example parametric plot of (x=sin(t),y=sin(t/3)) is shown below.

**Figure 7.9**
*Example Parametric Plot*

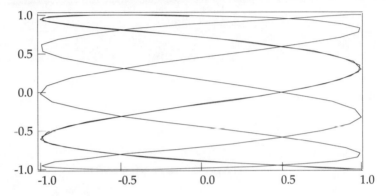

## 3D Scatter Plots

Figure 7.7 is a *2-dimensional scatter plot*, with *two* data locations and *one* data value. It is easy to extend the concept of scatter plots to three dimensions, where there are *three* data locations per data value.

In the example below we show two ways to visualize the same data: as three *1D* datasets or as a *single 3D* dataset.

Figure 7.10 is a table of the red, green, and blue relative values for five selected colors. We have arbitrarily assigned a color number to each of those five colors.

**Figure 7.10**
*Red, Green, Blue*
*Values for 5 Colors*

| Color | Color # | Red | Green | Blue |
|---|---|---|---|---|
| Canary | 0 | 0.470 | 0.470 | 0.060 |
| Orange | 1 | 0.700 | 0.260 | 0.040 |
| Brown | 2 | 0.400 | 0.400 | 0.200 |
| White | 3 | 0.330 | 0.330 | 0.330 |
| Violet | 4 | 0.490 | 0.020 | 0.490 |

What are the data values, the data locations, and the dimensionality of this dataset? One way of answering that question is shown below.

| Data Values | Red |
| --- | --- |
| | Green |
| | Blue |
| Data Location | Color Number |
| Data Description | RGB relative values (out of 1) for 5 selected colors |

A linegraph of the three 1-D datasets is shown in Figure 7.12.

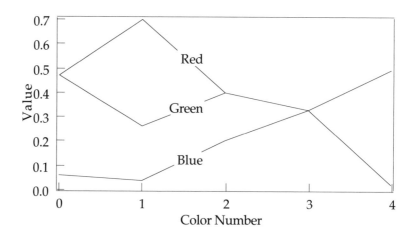

Another way to describe this data is as a single 3D dataset, shown below.

| Data Value | Color Number |
| --- | --- |
| Data Location | Red |
| | Green |
| | Blue |
| Data Description | RGB relative values (out of 1) for 5 selected colors |

A single 3D scatter plot of the dataset is shown in Figure 7.14.

Figure 7.14
Color Number vs.
Red, Green, Blue

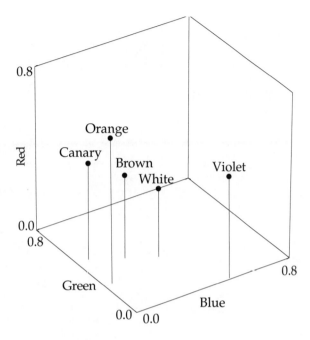

*Always decide which columns are values and which are locations before analyzing or graphing your data.*

In summary, the data shown in Figure 7.10 can be thought of as *three 1-dimensional* datasets (Figures 7.11 and 7.12) or as *one 3-dimensional* dataset (Figures 7.13 and 7.14). Although Figures 7.12 and 7.14 look very different, they are both visualizing exactly the same data.

Which way is correct? Both are, of course. Which organization you choose will depend on your needs. You may even want to change the way you organize the data in the middle of your analysis. But you should always keep track of your decision.

## Beyond Three Dimensions

Is it possible to graph column data that has more than three dimensions? The answer is yes, as the following example illustrates.

**Jeanne Beeker** has tested the solubility of 72 compounds in six different solvents. The first few lines of her data are shown in Figure 7.15.

**Figure 7.15**
*Solubility of Compounds in 6 Solvents*

| Compound | ETH | OCT | CCL4 | C6C6 | HEX | CHCL3 |
|---|---|---|---|---|---|---|
| METHANOL | -1.150 | -0.770 | -2.100 | -1.890 | -2.800 | -1.260 |
| ETHANOL | -0.570 | -0.310 | -1.400 | -1.620 | -2.100 | -0.850 |
| PROPANOL | -0.020 | 0.250 | -0.820 | -0.700 | -1.520 | -0.400 |
| BUTANOL | 0.890 | 0.880 | -0.400 | -0.120 | -0.700 | 0.450 |
| PENTANOL | 1.200 | 1.560 | 0.400 | 0.620 | -0.400 | 1.050 |
| HEXANOL | 1.800 | 2.030 | 0.990 | 1.300 | 0.460 | 1.690 |
| HEPTANOL | 2.400 | 2.410 | 1.670 | 1.910 | 1.010 | 2.410 |
| ACETIC ACID | -0.340 | -0.170 | -2.450 | -2.260 | -3.060 | -1.600 |
| • | • | • | • | • | • | • | • |

Jeanne first tried to think of her data as six 1D datasets, organized as shown in Figure 7.16.

**Figure 7.16**
*One Way to Organize Figure 7.15*

| Data Values | ETH, OCT, CCL4, C6C6, HEX, CHCL3 |
|---|---|
| Data Location | Compound |
| Data Description | Solubility of 72 compounds in 6 solvents |

She then graphed the solubility data values versus compound, shown in Figure 7.17. There are six lines in this linegraph, each line corresponding to one of the six solvents.

**Figure 7.17**
*Solubility vs. Compound*

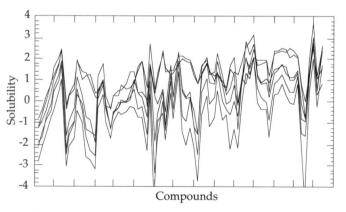

She did not feel she gained any insight from Figure 7.17. Next, she organized her data as one *6-dimensional* dataset.

**Figure 7.18**
*Another Way to Organize
Figure 7.15*

| Data Value | Compound |
|---|---|
| Data Locations | ETH, OCT, CCL4, C6C6, HEX, CHCL3 |
| Data Description | Solubility of 72 compounds in 6 solvents |

This created a problem. How do you graph a 6-dimensional dataset? (6-dimensional computer displays are hard to come by....)

Jeanne decided to use a *scatter matrix plot* for her 6-dimensional data[*]: every combination of one dimension vs. another dimension is plotted. So a 6-dimensional scatter plot is approximated by 6 × 6, or 36, 2-dimensional scatter plots.

In her case, each scatter plot has a solvent for the horizontal axis (the name in the same column) and a solvent for the vertical axis (the name in the same row). For example, the scatter plot in the upper right corner is the solvent CHCL3 (horizontal axis) vs. ETH (vertical axis) .

**Figure 7.19**
*Scatter Matrix Plot
for Figure 7.15*

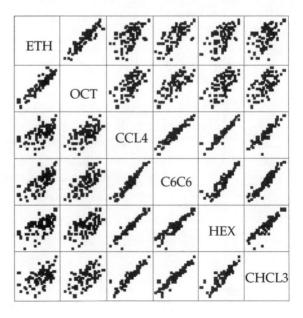

_____

[*] Figure 7.19 was produced using Systat.

The plots of a solvent against itself (HEX vs. HEX) are not shown, as they do not present any information. Also, the plots in the upper right half of this matrix (divided diagonally along the label cells) mirror the plots in the lower left half.

*It is often fruitful to play with selections for data values and locations to help in analysis.*

Note that information in five of the scatter plots forms distinctly diagonal patterns, which implies that the solubility of compounds in these solvents is highly correlated. It would be difficult to deduce the same information from Figure 7.17, although both are graphs of the same data.

### An Observation on Good Graphs

*For data locations, try to use numerical columns.*

There is a notable difference between the graphs that give good information (Figures 7.5, 7.7, 7.14, 7.19) and those that do not work as well (Figures 7.12, 7.17). The graphs in the latter category attempt to treat non-numerical columns such as color, compound, solvent, etc., as data *locations*. Data locations are best chosen from columns that are inherently numerical, such as X,Y map coordinates, solubility, etc.

## Summary

In this chapter we have discussed different ways of presenting column data: linegraphs and bar charts, scatter plots and parametric plots, and 3D scatter plots. You have seen that the same data can be represented in different dimensions to aid in analysis and visualization. Finally, the point was made that data locations are best chosen from columns that are inherently numerical.

# CHAPTER 8
# 2D MATRIX DATA

## Overview

The best way to store 2-dimensional data that fits on a regular grid is as a 2D matrix datafile. In this chapter we define what we mean by a regular grid, discuss how 2D matrix files are stored on disk, and then detail the various ways that 2D matrix data can be visualized.

## 2D Matrix Datafiles on Disk

We start with an example ASCII text column dataset repeated from Chapter 6.

*Figure 8.1*
*Column Data Example*

| X | Y | Velocity |
|---|---|----------|
| 0.5 | 0.5 | 0.0350 |
| 0.5 | 1.0 | 0.0714 |
| 0.5 | 1.5 | 0.3853 |
| 1.0 | 0.5 | 0.4911 |
| 1.0 | 1.0 | 0.2422 |
| 1.0 | 1.5 | 0.9207 |
| 1.5 | 0.5 | 0.5744 |
| 1.5 | 1.0 | 0.3305 |
| 1.5 | 1.5 | 0.8485 |

As we saw in Chapter 6, this dataset can be stored as a 2D matrix, shown below.

*Figure 8.2*
*2D Matrix for Velocity*

| | | X | | |
|---|---|---|---|---|
| | | 0.5 | 1.0 | 1.5 |
| Y | 0.5 | 0.0350 | 0.4911 | 0.5744 |
| | 1.0 | 0.0714 | 0.2422 | 0.3305 |
| | 1.5 | 0.3853 | 0.9207 | 0.8485 |

In Figure 8.2, the X, Y coordinates for a particular data value are given implicitly by the position of that data value in the matrix.

In Figure 8.1, we needed $9 \times 3 = 27$ numbers to represent the dataset. Figure 8.2 needed only $9+3+3=15$ numbers to represent the same data. As the arrays get bigger, the difference in disk space between the two schemes becomes even greater.[*]

Both Figures 8.1 and 8.2 code for a 2-dimensional dataset. However, we use the term *2D matrix* for Figure 8.2 to emphasize the fact that the data is also *stored* as a 2D array.

A column dataset can have any dimensionality because it can have any number of columns. A single 2D matrix dataset is always 2D, with two data locations for every data value.

A grayscale plot of this sample dataset is shown below.

**Figure 8.3**
*Grayscale Plot of
Velocity Data in Figure 8.2*

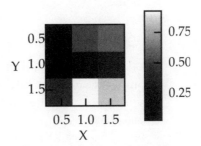

The data in Figure 8.2 was extracted from a much larger dataset of **Judy ReSyrch**'s work on the air flow through a fan.  A grayscale image of the full dataset is shown in Figure 8.24.

## An Example of a 2D Matrix Datafile

The actual disk file for a 2D matrix dataset will usually consist of a 2D matrix of the data values, two 1D arrays to hold the X and Y location values (often called *numerical scales*), and auxiliary information. For example, the ASCII 'Special' format used by Spyglass Transform stores the data in Figure 8.2 as the following.

---

[*] More generally, for an n×m array it takes $3 \times n \times m$ values to store 2D dataset as a column dataset, but only $n \times m + n + m$ values to store a 2D dataset as a 2D matrix dataset.

**Figure 8.4**
*ASCII 'Special' Version of Figure 8.2*

| Line # | Dataset | | | Comments |
|---|---|---|---|---|
| 1 | 3 | 3 | | Matrix Size |
| 2 | 0.92 | 0.03 | | Data Max/Min |
| 3 | 0.5 | 1.0 | 1.5 | Y Numerical Scales |
| 4 | 0.5 | 1.0 | 1.5 | X Numerical Scales |
| 5 | 0.0350 | 0.4911 | 0.5744 | Data |
| 6 | 0.0714 | 0.2422 | 0.3305 | Data |
| 7 | 0.3853 | 0.9207 | 0.8485 | Data |

(Only the numbers inside the box in Figure 8.4 are stored on disk. We added the other comments for clarity.) The 1D arrays for X and Y values are shown in lines 3 and 4, and the 2D data array is shown in lines 5, 6, and 7.

## ASCII Text and Binary 2D Matrix Datafiles

Most column datafiles follow the same format of header, titles, numbers separated by delimiters, and records divided by line separators. Column datafiles that follow this format are reasonably *self-describing*, meaning that no outside information is needed to read the file.

There is no standard layout for 2D matrix files, so it is almost impossible to create a self-describing 2D matrix datafile. Therefore, most 2D matrix datafiles are stored in binary form in pre-defined formats such as HDF, netCDF, FITS, or TIFF (see Chapters 12 and 13). Most ASCII text 2D matrix datafiles are stored in a private, self-defined format.

The one exception to this would be an ASCII text 2D matrix file that contains only data values, with *no* data locations. In that case, delimiters such as tabs, spaces, or commas can separate columns of numbers, and line separators can separate rows of numbers. This case is discussed more in the section on grids below.

## Row-Major vs. Column-Major Order

When writing your own 2D matrix file, you should know whether your computer and compiler store matrices in *row-major* or *column-major* order (since the 'matrix' is actually stored as a *sequence* of numbers). In row-major programs, all data elements for the first row are stored, then all data elements for the second row, and so on.

In column-major programs, all data elements for the first *column* are stored first. For example, consider this code segment:

**Figure 8.5**
*Code Segment for Array Order Example*

```
REAL A(2,3)
A(1,1)=1.2
A(1,2)=3.4
A(1,3)=5.6
A(2,1)=7.8
A(2,2)=9.10
A(2,3)=11.12
WRITE (*,*) A
```

In Figure 8.5, *row* refers to the first index of the array, and *column* refers to the second index. On *row-major* computer-compiler combinations, the output will look like the following.

**Figure 8.6**
*Row-Major Output from Figure 8.5*

| 1.2 | 3.4 | 5.6 |
|-----|------|-------|
| 7.8 | 9.10 | 11.12 |

On *column-major* computer-compiler combinations, the output will look like the following instead.

**Figure 8.7**
*Column-Major Output from Figure 8.5*

| 1.2 | 7.8 |
|-----|-------|
| 3.4 | 9.10 |
| 5.6 | 11.12 |

You need to be aware of the difference between row-major and column-major if you write your own 2D matrix files and transfer them between different computers. You may need to transpose, or flip end-for-end, your matrix on the destination computer.[*]

## Images as 2D Matrix Datafiles

*Images* and *photographs* are merely 2D matrix datafiles. When you take a black & white photograph, the camera records the view as intensity values on the film. These intensity values can be turned

[*] Spyglass Transform has an option to transpose arrays on import.

into a 2D matrix of numbers. You could visualize these numbers as a grayscale image, as we did above for a 2D matrix representing velocity data, but you could also visualize them as contour plots or surface plots.

A color photograph consists of *three* 2D matrix files, one each for red, green, and blue. A color image should not be confused with a *pseudocolor image*, where a *single* 2D matrix is visualized with colors. Pseudocolor imaging is described in the section on 2D visualization techniques below.

## Advantages of 2D Matrix Datafiles

Any data that can be stored as a 2D matrix dataset can also be stored as a column dataset. Why don't people use column datasets for everything? Some reasons are listed below.

> *2D matrix datasets take up much less disk space than column datasets for data on a regular 2-dimensional grid.*
>
> *2D matrix datasets* compress *better than corresponding column datasets. This is discussed in the section on sparse matrices below.*
>
> *Finding the data value at a particular (x, y) data location is easy for 2D matrix datasets. In column datasets, you may have to scan every datapoint to find the desired value.*
>
> *It is very easy to calculate the nearest neighbors of a particular data value on a 2D matrix.*
>
> *Useful visualization techniques such as contours, surface plots, and pseudocolor images* require *2D matrix datasets.*

## 2D Matrix Grids

First, we will explore the concept of uniform grids.

### Uniform Grids and No Grids

Our examples have all been of 2D matrix files with *uniform grids*. On a uniform grid the spacing of the X values is regular; the spacing of the Y values is also regular, although it does not have to be the same as the X value spacing. For example, a scatter plot of the data in Figure 8.2 is shown below.

*Figure 8.8*
*Scatter Plot for Figure 8.2*

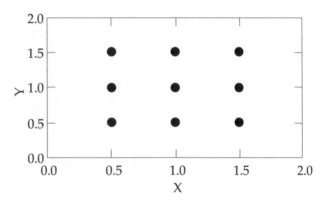

One of the justifications for 2D matrix datasets was to save disk space. With 2D matrix files on uniform grids, we can save even more disk space by getting rid of the X and Y numerical scales completely! They can be replaced with four numbers: the starting value for both X and Y, and the spacing of the X and Y numerical scales. These 2D matrix datafiles have *no grids*.

*For 'No Grid' files,*
*Row = Y Numerical Scale*
*Column = X Numerical Scale*

Many 2D matrix datafiles with no grids dispose with some or all of these four numbers that replace the grid. For example, *images* are 2D matrix files that rarely have grid information. In that case, the row and column numbers (1, 2, 3, 4, etc.) are used as the Y and X data locations respectively for the image.

Note that by tradition, the row number increases *downward*, whereas usually Y values increase *upward*. You need to be aware of this difference when dealing with 2D matrix files with *no grid*.

## Non-Uniform Grids

It is not necessary to have a uniform grid to store data as a 2D matrix datafile. Consider the 2D matrix datafile in Figure 8.9 below.

**Figure 8.9**
*2D Matrix for Velocity*

|   |     | X        |          |          |
|---|-----|----------|----------|----------|
|   |     | **0.5**  | **0.7**  | **1.8**  |
|   | **0.5** | 0.0350 | 0.4911 | 0.5744 |
| **Y** | **1.0** | 0.0714 | 0.2422 | 0.3305 |
|   | **1.1** | 0.3853 | 0.9207 | 0.8485 |

The 2D scatter plot for this dataset is shown below.

**Figure 8.10**
*Scatter Plot for Figure 8.9*

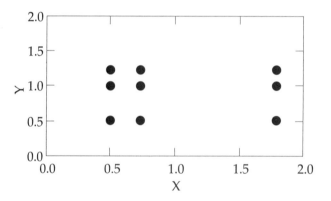

Clearly, this 2D matrix dataset does not have a uniform grid: the spacing between the X and Y numerical scales is not uniform. But it is a 2D matrix dataset, albeit with a *non-uniform grid*. We can store this data as a 2D matrix file because all numbers in a particular column have the same X value, and all numbers in a particular row have the same Y value.

A grayscale image of this data is shown below. Note that the Y axis in this figure increases *downward* (as in Figure 8.9), as opposed to Figure 8.10 where it increases *upward*.

**Figure 8.11**
*Grayscale Plot of Figure 8.9*

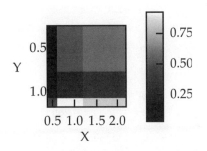

## Warped Grids

You may use the 2D matrix format even when the X and Y locations for every data value are different. Consider the following column datafile.

**Figure 8.12**
*Column Data Example of Warped Grid*

| X | Y | Velocity |
|-----|-----|----------|
| 0.5 | 0.5 | 0.0350 |
| 0.7 | 1.0 | 0.0714 |
| 0.5 | 1.5 | 0.3853 |
| 1.0 | 0.7 | 0.4911 |
| 1.0 | 1.0 | 0.2422 |
| 1.0 | 1.2 | 0.9207 |
| 1.5 | 0.5 | 0.5744 |
| 1.3 | 1.0 | 0.3305 |
| 1.5 | 1.5 | 0.8485 |

The scatter plot of this dataset is shown in Figure 8.13.

**Figure 8.13**
*Scatter Plot of Warped Grid Example*

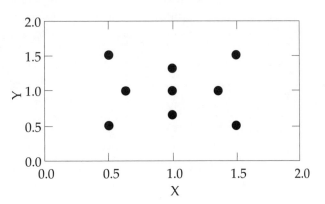

This dataset cannot be represented as either a 2D matrix with a uniform grid, or even a 2D matrix with a non-uniform grid. It can, however, be represented as a *warped* grid, shown below.

**Figure 8.14**
*2D Matrix with Warped Grid*

X

| | | |
|---|---|---|
| 0.0350 | 0.4911 | 0.5744 |
| (0.5,0.5) | (1.0,0.7) | (1.5,0.5) |
| 0.0714 | 0.2422 | 0.3305 |
| (0.7,1.0) | (1.0,1.0) | (1.3,1.0) |
| 0.3853 | 0.9207 | 0.8485 |
| (0.5,1.5) | (1.0,1.2) | (1.5,1.5) |

Y

In a warped (also known as a *rubber sheet*) grid, every data value has associated with it an (X,Y) pair of data locations. Why would someone store data this way instead of as a column dataset when there is clearly no disk savings?

The answer is that, except for disk space, warped grid files still offer all the advantages of 2D matrix files mentioned earlier, such as rapid access to data values, known nearest neighbors, and suitability for the use of 2D matrix visualization techniques.

2D matrix warped grid datafiles are similar in organization to polygonal datafiles, discussed in Chapter 10.

## Sparse Grids

Sometimes it is advantageous to store data as a 2D matrix even when you do not have data values for every (X,Y) location. Consider the following column datafile.

**Figure 8.15**
*Column Data Example of Sparse Grids*

| X | Y | Velocity |
|---|---|---|
| 0.5 | 1.0 | 0.0714 |
| 0.5 | 1.5 | 0.3853 |
| 1.0 | 0.5 | 0.4911 |
| 1.0 | 1.0 | 0.2422 |
| 1.5 | 0.5 | 0.5744 |
| 1.5 | 1.5 | 0.8485 |

The scatter plot of this dataset is shown in Figure 8.16.

**Figure 8.16**
*Scatter Plot of*
*Sparse Grid Example*

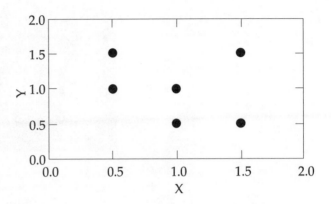

The datafile looks like it fits on a uniform grid, but with some missing values. We can store this file as a 2D matrix; it would look like the following.

**Figure 8.17**
*2D Matrix for*
*Sparse Grid Example*

| | | X | |
|---|---|---|---|
| | **0.5** | **1.0** | **1.5** |
| **0.5** | NaN | 0.4911 | 0.5744 |
| **1.0** | 0.0714 | 0.2422 | NaN |
| **1.5** | 0.3853 | NaN | 0.8485 |

(Y labels the rows: 0.5, 1.0, 1.5)

We have placed a NaN at matrix locations that do not have a value. 2D matrices like Figure 8.17 contain *missing data values*. They are called *sparse matrices*.

For example, **Dr. Mike Astroe** wondered what went wrong with his FITS image. He had first read in a 2D matrix file representing an X-ray photograph of the Crab pulsar. He then generated a grayscale image of the dataset, shown in Figure 8.18.

**Figure 8.18**
*Grayscale Image of 2D*
*FITS File with Missing Data*

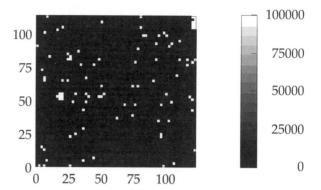

This was nothing like the image he anticipated, so he took a closer look at the data. A small sample is shown below.

**Figure 8.19**
*Sample of Astroe*
*FITS File Data*

|  |  | X | | |
|---|---|---|---|---|
|  |  | **104** | **105** | **106** |
|  | **59** | 5.101 | 3.700 | 3.101 |
|  | **60** | 4.400 | 4.101 | 4.700 |
| **Y** | **61** | 4.050 | 4.298 | 4.149 |
|  | **62** | 99999.992 | 4.251 | 3.700 |
|  | **63** | 2.801 | 99999.992 | 4.349 |
|  | **64** | 4.050 | 4.400 | 4.601 |

What are those 99999 numbers? This datafile uses 99999 as the value for missing numbers (also called *outliers*). The program generating the grayscale image interpreted outliers as actual data points and scaled the grayscale values between 0 and 99999. To correct the problem Mike instructed the imaging program to ignore the outliers. This generated the image shown in Figure 8.20.

**Figure 8.20**
*Grayscale Image of a 2D*
*FITS File with Missing Data*
*Scaled Appropriately*

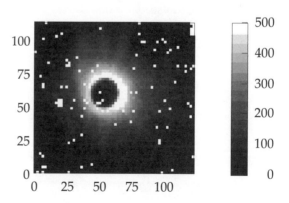

The white spots on the image represent the missing values. In Chapter 11 we discuss ways to remove these—a necessary step before using 2D visualization techniques such as surface plots and contour plots.

## The Dimensionality of 2D Matrix Data

### 2D Matrix Files as Column Files

You could interpret Figure 8.2 as a column dataset. In that case the datafile would consist of four columns: a Y column, an X=0.5 column, an X=1.0 column, and an X=1.5 column. You would then naturally interpret the datafile as *three 1-dimensional* datasets. A linegraph of these three datasets is shown below.

**Figure 8.21**
*Plotting Figure 8.2 as Three 1D Datasets*

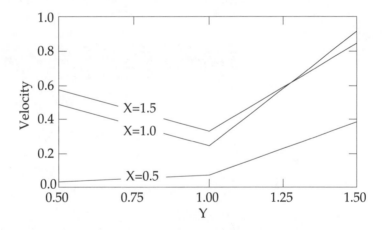

Note that no use is being made of X as a location variable. The data is intrinsically 2-dimensional, and should be treated as such. Compare this image with Figure 8.3, which is a visualization of the same data.

### Column Files as 2D Matrix Files

It is also possible to consider a column datafile as a 2D matrix file. For example, **Dr. Jeanne Beeker**'s data from Chapter 7, Figure 7.15, consists of one column for compound name, and six columns for the solubility data for the six solvents. We can assign a number to each

compound and each solvent, thereby creating a 6 x 72 2D matrix
dataset.

**Figure 8.22**
*Data from Figure 7.15*
*Evaluated as a*
*2D Matrix File*

| Compound # | Solvent Number | | | | | |
|---|---|---|---|---|---|---|
| | 1 | 2 | 3 | 4 | 5 | 6 |
| 1 | -1.150 | -0.770 | -2.100 | -1.890 | -2.800 | -1.260 |
| 2 | -0.570 | -0.310 | -1.400 | -1.620 | -2.100 | -0.850 |
| 3 | -0.020 | 0.250 | -0.820 | -0.700 | -1.520 | -0.400 |
| 4 | 0.890 | 0.880 | -0.400 | -0.120 | -0.700 | 0.450 |
| 5 | 1.200 | 1.560 | 0.400 | 0.620 | -0.400 | 1.050 |
| 6 | 1.800 | 2.030 | 0.990 | 1.300 | 0.460 | 1.690 |
| 7 | 2.400 | 2.410 | 1.670 | 1.910 | 1.010 | 2.410 |
| 8 | -0.340 | -0.170 | -2.450 | -2.260 | -3.060 | -1.600 |
| • | • | • | • | • | • | • |

A 2D grayscale plot of this dataset (solubility as a function of
solvent number and compound number) is shown below.

**Figure 8.23**
*Grayscale Plot of*
*Data in Figure 8.22*

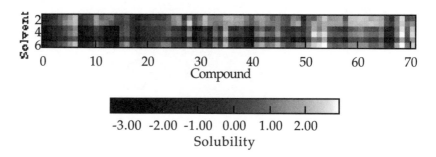

Note that we have flipped the X and Y axes for this plot so it will
fit on the page. In this plot you can find compounds that are soluble
in most solvents by looking for all white columns; find the solvents
that don't dissolve any of the compounds by looking for dark rows.

Figures 7.17, 7.19, and 8.23 are all visualizations of the same data.
Each of them uses a different choice for the dimensionality of the
data, and each of them may be useful for seeing different features of
the data.

A personal preference of ours is to visualize data with as high a
dimensionality as possible (as in Figure 7.19, for example).

The Data Handbook

## Visualizing 2D Matrix Data

We give examples of the most popular 2D matrix visualization techniques below. *None* of these methods work with 2-dimensional column data. Column data must first be converted to 2D matrix using techniques described in Chapter 11.

### Color Raster Imaging

In *Color Raster Imaging*, the data values in the 2D matrix are converted into shades of gray or to colors to create a *grayscale* or *pseudocolor* image. In the image below from **Judy ReSyrch**'s project, high data values are converted to white, low data values to black, and intermediate values to appropriate shades of gray.

*Figure 8.24*
*Grayscale Plot of*
*Velocity Data*

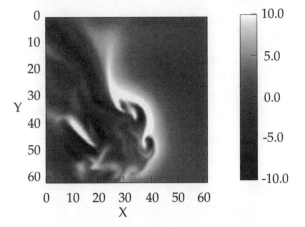

The 2D matrix is converted to a grayscale image by first scaling the data values to the range 0 to 255. These numbers are then used as indices into a *color table*, where the red, green, and blue values are used to show a color on the screen.

Each entry in the color table consists of three bytes: a byte for red intensity, a byte for green intensity, and a byte for blue intensity. The color black is coded as (0,0,0), white is (255,255,255), and dark red is (128,0,0).

In Figure 8.25, the data on the left has already been scaled from 0 to 255. A scaled value of 6 is being converted to a very dark gray (6,6,6) for display. The color table used in this figure is called grayscale.

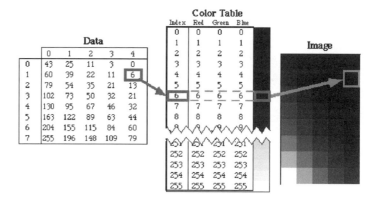

**Figure 8.25**
*Converting Numbers to Colors*

Color raster plots are good for giving an overall feel for the dataset, and for showing fine detail of the data. In particular, it is easy to pick out high and low values by looking for areas of light and dark.

**Color Raster Imaging**
*Good at overall feel, seeing Min/Max values, fine detail. Poor at quantitative information*

Color raster plots are not very good at giving quantitative information: you do not know beforehand what data value `red` represents, for example. This is why every grayscale image in this book also has a scale next to it, showing the mapping of numbers to gray levels. You will also see labeled contour plots (described below) placed on top of raster images to give that quantitative information.

Also, sometimes color raster images cannot be used, such as for publishing articles in journals that only accept line art. Also, color raster images are difficult to photocopy.

## Surface Plots

In surface plots the data values of the 2D matrix are converted to a height of a rubber membrane above a plane. A perspective view of this surface is then displayed on the screen. These plots are often called *3D plots*.  This term is misleading because, although the rubber membrane is a 3D object, the underlying data being visualized is 2-dimensional.

**Figure 8.26**
*Surface Plot of Velocity*

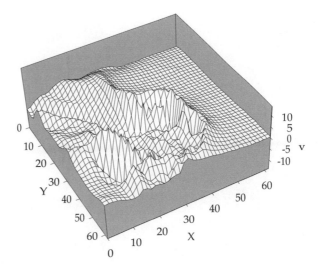

Surface plots can be generated very rapidly, and can be rotated and scaled for best viewing. A good surface plot can give you a rapid feel for the dataset, complete with quantitative information via the numerical labels for X, Y, and the data value. Surface plots are often the method of choice when grayscale or color images cannot be used (when publishing articles, for example).

**Surface Plots**
*Good at overall feel, quantitative information; poor at fine detail, may obscure features*

On the downside, there is a limit to the number of lines that can be used for the mesh without creating a big, black blob. This limit (about 100 lines per axis) means that it is difficult to show fine details on a surface plot. In addition, sometimes key features can be hidden by the folds of the surface itself.

## Contour Plots

In contour plots, used widely in mapping and for meteorological data, lines are generated to connect data points that have the same value. The method is identical to that used to generate topological maps, where lines represent altitude in feet.

In Figure 8.27, a contour plot of `velocity`, contours were drawn for every data value between -10 and 10, in increments of 2.5. Many of the contour lines are labeled. The dashed contour lines are for data values that are less than 0.

**Figure 8.27**
*Contour Plot of Velocity*

Contour plots with labels excel at showing you what the data values are at any point in the plot. Contour plots also make it easy to see where data values are changing rapidly, because the contour lines become very close to each other. And since contour plots consist of lines, they can be used in situations where you must have line art.

**Contour Plots**
*Good at quantitative information, slope information; poor at overall feel, labels may obscure details.*

One problem with contour plots is that it is difficult to get an overall feel for the data at a glance. You have to read the labels to see which contours represent high data values, and which represent low values. In addition, the labels themselves can sometimes hide fine features of the data.

## Vector Plots

All the datasets we have discussed so far have been *scalar* datasets, in the sense that only one data value at a particular data location is visualized (temperature, velocity, etc.). But suppose you have a *vector* dataset, with two or three components of a data value at each data location? In Figure 8.28, at each data location there are two data values, namely the X and the Y components of wind velocity.

The Data Handbook

**Figure 8.28**
*Vector Plot of Velocity
Overlay on Raster Image*

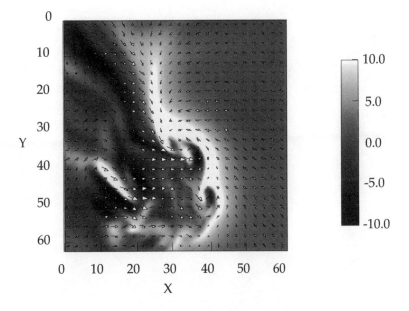

These two components are visualized as a *vector plot*, where the length of the vector at each data location is equal to $\sqrt{x^2+y^2}$ , and the direction of the vector is equal to $\tan^{-1}(y/x)$ . You can think of the arrows as pointing in the direction the wind is blowing, so to speak.

Vector plots are the most popular way to represent 2D matrix datasets that represent vectors. Vector plots also can be placed on raster images, as done above, to give information both on a scalar value (velocity magnitude) and on a vector value (velocity direction).

## Summary

We have shown how most 2-dimensional data can be stored as 2D matrix files. We discussed how 2D matrix files are stored on disk, and how 2D matrix data is gridded. Finally, we discussed some very powerful 2D matrix visualization techniques—so powerful it is worth putting up with the 'pain' sometimes required to use them.

# CHAPTER 9
# 3D MATRIX (VOLUMETRIC )DATA

## Overview

The best way to store *volumetric* data is as a 3D matrix file. In this chapter we define what we mean by volumetric data, show how 3D files are stored on disk, and detail the ways that 3D data can be visualized.

## 3D Matrix Datafiles on Disk

As we did in the previous chapter, we start with an example ASCII column dataset from Chapter 6.

*Figure 9.1*
*3D Column Data Example*

| X | Y | Z | Velocity |
|-----|-----|-----|----------|
| 0.5 | 0.5 | 0.0 | 0.0350 |
| 0.5 | 1.0 | 0.0 | 0.0714 |
| 0.5 | 1.5 | 0.0 | 0.3853 |
| 1.0 | 0.5 | 0.0 | 0.4911 |
| 1.0 | 1.0 | 0.0 | 0.2422 |
| 1.0 | 1.5 | 0.0 | 0.9207 |
| 1.5 | 0.5 | 0.0 | 1.6070 |
| 1.5 | 1.0 | 0.0 | 1.1980 |
| 1.5 | 1.5 | 0.0 | 0.8690 |
| 0.5 | 0.5 | 3.0 | 0.6250 |
| 0.5 | 1.0 | 3.0 | 0.4754 |
| 0.5 | 1.5 | 3.0 | 0.4043 |
| 1.0 | 0.5 | 3.0 | 0.3673 |
| 1.0 | 1.0 | 3.0 | 0.3096 |
| 1.0 | 1.5 | 3.0 | 0.1824 |
| 1.5 | 0.5 | 3.0 | 1.7672 |
| 1.5 | 1.0 | 3.0 | 1.7253 |
| 1.5 | 1.5 | 3.0 | 1.7757 |
| 0.5 | 0.5 | 6.0 | 1.1853 |
| 0.5 | 1.0 | 6.0 | 0.9144 |
| 0.5 | 1.5 | 6.0 | 0.7263 |
| 1.0 | 0.5 | 6.0 | 0.6164 |
| 1.0 | 1.0 | 6.0 | 0.5557 |
| 1.0 | 1.5 | 6.0 | 0.4966 |
| 1.5 | 0.5 | 6.0 | 2.4064 |
| 1.5 | 1.0 | 6.0 | 2.5157 |
| 1.5 | 1.5 | 6.0 | 2.7190 |

Since this dataset has a uniform grid (this time in X, Y, *and* Z) it can be stored as a 3D matrix.

We can represent a 3D matrix file as a deck of cards. Each card in the deck is a single 2D matrix file, with X and Y as the dimensions. Every card has a unique Z value. A schematic of this representation is shown in Figure 9.2.

**Figure 9.2**
*Representing a 3D Matrix File as a Card Deck*

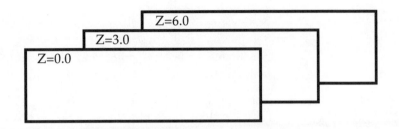

In Figure 9.3 we show the data from Figure 9.1 in 3D matrix format as a series of cards or layers.

**Figure 9.3**
*Data from Figure 9.1 Stored as a 3D Matrix File*

| Z=0.0 | | | | |
|---|---|---|---|---|
| | Z=3.0 | | | |
| | | Z=6.0 | 0.5 | 1.0 | 1.5 |

The table as displayed (layered):

| Z=6.0 | 0.5 | 1.0 | 1.5 | |
|---|---|---|---|---|
| Z=3.0 | 0.5 | 1.0 | 1.5 | 2.4064 |
| Z=0.0 | 0.5 | 1.0 | 1.5 | 1.7672 | 2.5157 |
| 0.5 | 0.0350 | 0.4911 | 0.5744 | 1.7253 | 2.7190 |
| 1.0 | 0.0714 | 0.2422 | 0.3305 | 1.7757 |
| 1.5 | 0.3853 | 0.9207 | 0.8485 |

The top layer is labeled Z=0.0. The Z=3.0 and Z=6.0 layers are partially obscured. The dataset in Figure 9.1 needs 27×3=81 numbers to store all of the data values. Storing the same data as a 3D matrix file requires 27+3+3+3=36 numbers.[*]

**Volumetric Data = 3D Matrix Data**

Data stored in a 3D matrix is often called *volumetric* data, because the numbers fill a volume. The actual disk file usually consists of the 3D matrix of values, three 1D arrays to hold the X, Y, and Z numerical scales, and auxiliary information such as a header.

## ASCII Text and Binary 3D Matrix Datafiles

As in the case of 2D matrix files, there is no standard layout for 3D matrix files. Therefore, many 3D matrix files are stored in binary. Different formats include HDF, ACR-NEMA, netCDF, etc.

---

[*] More generally, for an n×m×p array it takes 4×n×m×p values to store 3D dataset as a column dataset, but only n×m×p+n+m+p values to store a 3D dataset as a 3D matrix dataset.

3D matrix files tend to be very large. A small volumetric dataset of dimensions 100×100×100 contains one million data values! The datafile disk size would be two megabytes for short integers, four megabytes for floating point, and ~twelve megabytes for ASCII text.

*3D matrix simulations with multi-megabyte arrays are strongly encouraged by the Disk Drive Manufacturers Association...*

This disk space situation is one reason why 3D matrix files typically do not use ASCII text. Also, it can take a very long time to read in one million ASCII numbers. Because of these size issues, it is relatively common to use fixed-point bytes or short integers to store volumetric data. As described in Chapter 3, you must remember to scale these values before displaying them.

### 3D Matrix Grids

Because of the size and complexity of 3D matrix datasets, it is rare to see a 3D matrix file with anything other than a *uniform* grid. In fact, most people actually use *no grid*, and instead store six numbers of X,Y,Z starting value and X,Y,Z increment.

Therefore, if your original data is on a non-uniform grid, you have to *regrid* the data to a uniform grid for display and analysis. In Chapter 11 we discuss some methods of regridding data.

## The Dimensionality of 3D Matrix Data

### 3D Matrix File from a Series of 2D Matrix Files

**Dr. Tim Boans** has a series of 2D matrix files that represented MRI (<u>M</u>agnetic <u>R</u>esonance <u>I</u>maging) scans of a colleague. Two of the scans are shown in Figure 9.4.

*Figure 9.4*
*Two MRI Scans*

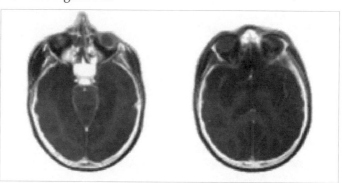

Tim has 54 of these images. He loaded the scans into an animation program and played them back and forth for hours. But Dr. Boans wondered if there was another way to look at the data.

He combined the images into a single 3D matrix dataset. Every 2D image was then like a card in the card deck , as seen below.

**Figure 9.5**
*MRI Scans as a Card Deck*

(Note that the images in Figure 9.5 have been rotated 180° with respect to the original images in Figure 9.4.) Next Dr. Boans loaded the 3D matrix into a volumetric visualization program and produced the image seen in Figure 9.6.

**Figure 9.6**
*Volumetric Rendering of MRI Scans*

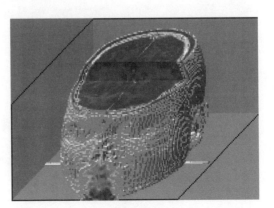

The rendering in Figure 9.6 gives an overall feel for the datasets, and the individual slices in Figure 9.4 give the fine level of detail sometimes needed.

## Series of 2D Matrix Files from a 3D Matrix File

We have been talking about the 3D matrix dataset as a card deck, with each 2D image being a card in the deck. Imagine now separating the cards, *but in a different direction*.

**Figure 9.7**
*3D Matrix as a Card Deck in a Perpendicular Direction*

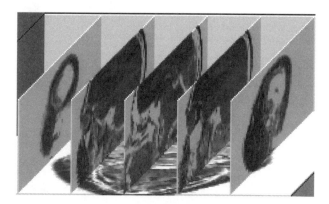

In Figure 9.7 above, Dr. Boans created a series of 2D matrix images going *left to right* from the 3D matrix. Recall that the 3D matrix was originally created by combining a series of 2D matrix images going *bottom to top*.

Two of these new 2D matrix images are displayed below. The resolution of these images is less than that seen in Figure 9.4 because each original MRI image was 128 x 128 , but in the images below the vertical resolution is only 54 (because of the 54 original images).

**Figure 9.8**
*Two New MRI Scans Created from 3D Matrix*

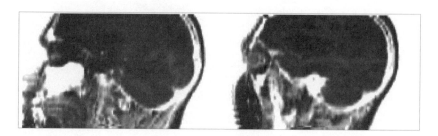

In summary, turning a 2D matrix series into a 3D matrix file, or turning a 3D matrix file into a 2D matrix series, is a powerful technique that can often help you analyze and visualize your data.

## Visualizing 3D Matrix Data

Visualizing 3D matrix data used to be almost impossible for the average scientist or engineer. 3D matrix visualization requires dealing with millions or hundreds of millions of numbers, and many of the standard 3D matrix visualization techniques require an inordinate amount of computer power.

Luckily, things have changed. Desktop computers have become vastly more powerful, and 3D matrix software has become easier to use. But there is no getting around the fact that 3D matrix visualization will always take more effort than 2D matrix or column visualization.

The standard 3D matrix visualization techniques of slicing/dicing, isosurfaces, volumetric rendering, and streamlines are described below.[*]

### Slice/Dice

To describe *slicing and dicing*, we once again return to the idea of a 3D matrix file as a series of cards in a card deck. In slice/dice, selected cards (or *slices*) are displayed as grayscale or pseudocolor images, and then placed in perspective in a cube that represents the boundary of the 3D matrix dataset. These slices can be cut from any direction: $(X,Y)$, $(X,Z)$, or $(Y,Z)$.

For example, **Judy ReSyrch** selected four $(X,Y)$ 2D matrix slices in a 3D matrix representing the pressure variable from her 3D simulation of airflow through a fan. She generated a color raster image for each slice, then positioned each slice in a perspective view to produce the following image.

---

[*] All images in this chapter were generated with Spyglass Dicer, except for Figure 9.16 (VoxelView).

---

**Figure 9.9**
*Four Slices from 3D Matrix
Representing Pressure*

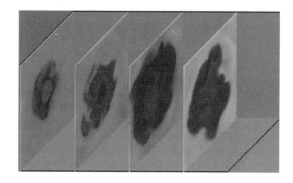

Judy then added a single slice from each of the (X,Z) and (Y,Z) planes to produce the image below.

**Figure 9.10**
*Perpendicular Slices
from 3D Matrix
Representing Pressure*

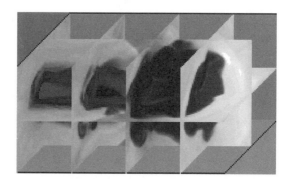

In some areas of Figure 9.10 it is difficult to discern what slice a particular feature is on. To get around this, Dr. ReSyrch added *differential shading* to the slices, shown below.

**Figure 9.11**
*Perpendicular slices
from 3D Matrix
Representing Pressure
with Differential Shading*

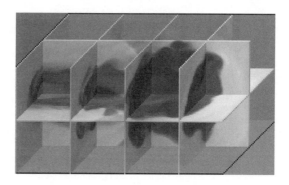

The slices are differentially shaded by modifying the lightness of each slice depending on which direction it is facing. This can give a good illusion of perspective.

Finally, Judy used *transparency* on the image. In this technique, a selected data range is 'shown' as transparent rather than a color.

**Figure 9.12**
*Slices with Transparency from 3D Matrix Representing Pressure*

Slicing/dicing is a very powerful technique. It is also the fastest (by far) of the common 3D matrix visualization methods. It shares all of the strengths of 2D matrix color raster imaging (see Chapter 8)—which is to say, it is great at detail and at showing min/max information.

**Slicing and Dicing**
*Great at detail, very fast, interactive; possible to miss features, hard to see 3D shapes.*

The downside is that each slice is positioned by hand. Therefore, it is possible to miss an important feature by not positioning a slice in an appropriate position. It is also difficult to construct the 3D shape of an embedded object, such as the pressure jet shown above.

## Isosurfaces

Contour plots are one of the most popular 2D matrix visualization techniques. In a contour plot, contour lines connect equal data values.

For example, in Figure 8.27 the line marked 10.0 connects all data values that equal 10.0. Where there are no data values exactly equal to 10.0, the contouring routine will interpolate between values higher than and lower than 10.0, to show where a data value of 10.0 would be if there were more datapoints.

These contour lines are also known as *isolines*: lines that represent a single data value. In a 3D matrix, it takes not a line but a *surface* to connect data values that are equal. This connecting surface is known, not surprisingly, as an *isosurface*. An example is shown below.

**Figure 9.13**
*Isosurface of Pressure Jet*

As with slicing/dicing, an isosurface needs to be shaded to give a sense of three-dimensional perspective. Without shading, all you would see is a single blob of color, with no clues regarding shape. Generating the isosurfaces and the isosurface shading used to take a very large amount of computer power. Recently, however, new techniques have speeded things up. For example, the image in Figure 9.13 took about a 30 seconds to generate on a Macintosh Quadra 700.

Isosurfaces are very popular because they rapidly give a good overall feel for the three-dimensional shape of the data. They can make the flow of a fluid seem almost real. But (of course) there is a problem.

**Isosurfaces**
*Good at 3-dimensional shape of data; can only show one level at a time.*

A fundamental difference between contour plots and isosurfaces is that with contour plots, you can have many contour levels drawn on the same plot. With isosurfaces, however, you are pretty much limited to a single contour level. All information about data values above and below the contour level is lost.

One way to get around this problem is to combine isosurfaces with slices/dices, as shown below.

**Figure 9.14**
*Isosurface with Two Slices*

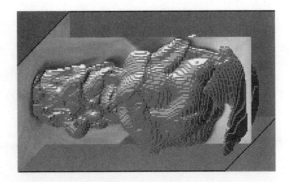

In this rendering you still cannot see inside the isosurface. It is possible, however to *cut into* the surface, so to speak, to render parts of the inside of the isosurface. An example of this is shown below.

**Figure 9.15**
*Isosurface with Two Slices and a Cutout*

In summary, combining slicing/dicing with isosurfacing can give you great insight into your 3D matrix data. But keep in mind that creating good images of 3D matrix data and analyzing it takes longer than it would for column data or 2D matrix data.

## Volumetric Visualization

Another 3D matrix visualization technique is called *volumetric visualization*. The use of this term is somewhat confusing, since many people use it to refer to all 3D matrix visualization techniques. In volumetric visualization, each data value is converted to an *intensity*. Every data value intensity is then plotted, mostly on top of each other. If one data value intensity plots on top of another data value intensity, the intensities are added together in some fashion, as shown in the image below.

*Figure 9.16*
*Volumetric Visualization*
*of a Heart*

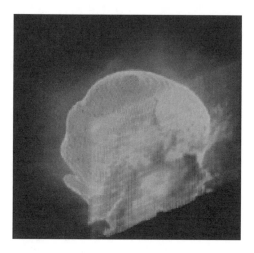

Volumetric visualization is conceptually much easier than it sounds. Look at a cloud, for instance. Where the water vapor density is very high, the cloud is *opaque*. Where the water vapor density is very low, the cloud is *transparent*. In intermediate regions, the cloud is *translucent* (you can partially see through it).

Nature illustrates the 3-dimensional distribution of water vapor by the *opacity* of the cloud. Volumetric visualization mimics nature by creating a 'cloud' of your data. Where all data values are low along a line of sight, you can see through the data. Where the data values are high, you cannot see through it.

In volumetric visualization, unlike any other 3D matrix visualization process, *all* data values are plotted. Because of this, volumetric visualization excels at providing complete overall information on your data. But this strength is also a weakness. With so much data, it takes great skill on your part to select the right opacities and colors; failure to do so may result in the formation of a big blob.

**Volumetric Visualization**
*Shows all of the data, good at overall shape; excellent animations; requires high level of skill, lots of computer power .*

Volumetric visualization images have few perspective clues like shading to help you figure out the 3-dimensional shape of the data. Because of this, it is common to *animate* a series of volumetric visualization images by spinning the data volume. This animation provides the visual clues needed to figure out the 3D shape of the data.

Generating a single volumetric visualization image takes somewhat more computer power than a single isosurface image. And since most volumetric visualizations are animations, the total computational burden is very high. But with enough skill and with big enough computers, you can construct very insightful images using volumetric visualization.

## Vector Fields and Streamlines

2D matrix vector fields can be graphed with 2D vector plots; 3D matrix vector fields can be graphed with 3D vector plots. However, each vector can now point in any direction in three dimensions, not just two. Also, each vector can be positioned anywhere in three dimensions. Discerning what direction each vector points and where each vector is positioned in 3D space is a real challenge.

One way to handle this is to use slicing/dicing to choose 2D planes for drawing vector plots. However, in order to draw the vectors on that slice, you have to assume that the vectors are 2-dimensional, not 3-dimensional. This means discarding information.

Another way to visualize 3D vector fields is through the use of streamlines. Streamlines are similar to throwing smoke bombs in a windstorm. A windstorm defines a 3D vector field of wind velocity (north-south wind speed, east-west wind speed, vertical wind speed). The smoke bomb traces out a path in that 3D vector field (ignore gravity in this thought experiment).

A streamline is a computerized version of the smoke bombs. Each streamline is a line drawn in three dimensions tracing the path a particle would take through the data, if the data represented wind velocity.

Once again, there are few depth clues to tell where those lines actually *are* in 3-dimensional space. Because of that, streamline plots are usually animated by rotation, in the same way that volumetric visualization images are.

## Summary

3D matrix files are much larger and more complex than 2D matrix files, because of the extra dimension. However, virtually all 3D matrix files have uniform grids. It is often very useful to visualize a 2D matrix file series as a 3D matrix file, and vice versa.

The most popular 3D matrix visualization techniques are slicing/dicing, isosurfaces, and volumetric visualization. None of these methods is ideal, and all require more computer power and skill than their 2D matrix counterparts.

# CHAPTER 10
# POLYGONAL DATA

## Overview

Sometimes *polygonal data* is the best way to store data of simulations or observations. In this chapter we explain what we mean by polygonal data, show ways that polygonal data is organized, and discuss some of its uses.

## Unstructured Grids vs. Structured Grids

Polygonal data is always organized on an *unstructured* grid. To understand an unstructured grid, first consider a *structured* grid.

### Structured Grids

All the grids discussed in Chapters 6 and 8 (uniform grids, non-uniform grids, warped grids) are known collectively as *structured grids*. In a structured grid, it is very easy to find the nearest neighbors of every data value in the grid. Consider the example of a warped grid from Chapter 8, repeated below.

*Figure 10.1*
*2D Matrix with*
*Warped Grid*

|   |   | X 1 | 2 | 3 |
|---|---|------|------|------|
|   | 1 | 0.0350 (0.5,0.5) | 0.4911 (1.0,0.7) | 0.5744 (1.5,0.5) |
| Y | 2 | 0.0714 (0.7,1.0) | 0.2422 (1.0,1.0) | 0.3305 (1.3,1.0) |
|   | 3 | 0.3853 (0.5,1.5) | 0.9207 (1.0,1.2) | 0.8485 (1.5,1.5) |

In Figure 10.1 we have added row and column index numbers to the X and Y scales. These index numbers are *not* the data locations. In this example the data locations are stored with every data value. The index numbers provide us with access to the numbers on the computer. Referring to the (row, column) index numbers of (2,2) will give the data value of 0.2422 and the data locations of (1.0,1.0).

*Structured Grids*
*Nearest neighbors implicitly given by position in storage array.*

The nearest neighbors of (2,2) are (2,1), (1,2), (2,3), and (3,2). We did not need to search the dataset for the nearest data locations. All we had to do was to add 1 or subtract 1 from the row and column indices, and the nearest neighbors fell into our lap.

## Unstructured Grids

Sometimes it is impossible to organize data as any type of structured grid. Imagine trying to model the reaction of an automobile to an impact with an immovable object. No amount of warping of a 2D matrix or a 3D matrix would be sufficient to make an accurate model of the hood, the windshield, the roof, the doors, the seats, etc. Researchers performing these types of calculations use instead *unstructured* grids.

In an unstructured grid, every data value contains information not only on its data locations, but also on its *nearest neighbors*. The figure below is identical to Figure 10.1 except that we have removed the index values and have added arbitrary index numbers to every data value.

*Figure 10.2*
*2D Matrix with*
*Warped Grid*
*and Index Numbers*

|   | X | | |
|---|---|---|---|
|   | **1**<br>0.0350<br>(0.5,0.5) | **4**<br>0.4911<br>(1.0,0.7) | **7**<br>0.5744<br>(1.5,0.5) |
| Y | **2**<br>0.0714<br>(0.7,1.0) | **5**<br>0.2422<br>(1.0,1.0) | **8**<br>0.3305<br>(1.3,1.0) |
|   | **3**<br>0.3853<br>(0.5,1.5) | **6**<br>0.9207<br>(1.0,1.2) | **9**<br>0.8485<br>(1.5,1.5) |

In Figure 10.3 , we turn this 2D matrix dataset back into a column dataset, but with two new columns. The first column just lists the arbitrary index numbers we have added for every data value.

*Figure 10.3*
*Unstructured Grid Example*

| Index | X | Y | Velocity | Neighbors |
|---|---|---|---|---|
| 1 | 0.5 | 0.5 | 0.0350 | 2,4 |
| 2 | 0.7 | 1.0 | 0.0714 | 1,3,5 |
| 3 | 0.5 | 1.5 | 0.3853 | 2,6 |
| 4 | 1.0 | 0.7 | 0.4911 | 1,5,7 |
| 5 | 1.0 | 1.0 | 0.2422 | 2,4,6,8 |
| 6 | 1.0 | 1.2 | 0.9207 | 3,5,9 |
| 7 | 1.5 | 0.5 | 0.5744 | 4,8 |
| 8 | 1.3 | 1.0 | 0.3305 | 5,7,9 |
| 9 | 1.5 | 1.5 | 0.8485 | 6,8 |

The last column is the interesting one. It lists the index values of the nearest neighbors for every data value. This is, in fact, an example of an *unstructured grid*, where every data value carries information not only on data locations, but also on its nearest neighbors.

**Unstructured Grids**
*Every data value contains data locations and nearest neighbor information.*

In the warped grid example (Figure 10.1), the location of the data value in the (row, column) array *implicitly* tells you what the data value's nearest neighbors are. This is the reason we stored the warped grid data as a 2D matrix dataset in the first place, even though it took up as much disk space as the corresponding column dataset.

But in unstructured grids, the list of nearest neighbors is *explicit*. There is no need to use the matrix to define the nearest neighbor. Because of this, unstructured grid data is *always* stored in column form as opposed to matrix.

## Node-Based Data vs. Cell-Based Data

The unstructured grid example shown in Figure 10.3 is of a *node-based* dataset: one in which the *data values* are defined at the *data locations* (known here as *nodes*). This might seem a little silly. Where else would the data values be defined? Aren't data values always defined at the data locations? Not always.

In *cell-based* datasets, the data values are defined not at the data locations, but in a *cell*: some sort of object, usually a *polygon*. A polygon here means a closed surface defined by a series of nodes, or data locations. An example is shown below.

**Figure 10.4**
*Polygonal Cell Example*

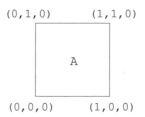

In this example, the cell labeled A is a polygonal cell with four nodes (sometimes known as *vertices*). The (X,Y,Z) values of each node are given in the figure. The data value is defined at the center of the cell, right where the A is.

This might seem like a lot of definitions and a lot of work. Why bother? Why not just keep the data values where the data locations are? Because the best way to store information on material things such as  cars, bridges, airplanes, etc. is as *polygons*. The polygon can represent a small segment of the sheet metal that makes up a wing, for example.

We just defined a bunch of words, some of them meaning the same thing. In the table below, words in the same column can be thought of as synonyms.

**Figure 10.5**
*Table of Synonyms*

| Object | Data Location | Cell-Based Unstructured Grid |
|--------|---------------|------------------------------|
| Cell | Node | Polygonal Data |
| Polygon | Vertex | |

Now we can define *polygonal data*: data stored on a cell-based unstructured grid, where in this case the cells are polygons. All unstructured grid data is organized as *columns*, not as 2D or 3D matrices.

## Polygonal Data on Disk

A polygonal dataset usually consists of two lists. The first list is the list of nodes; the second is the list of polygons. Associated with each polygon is the list of nodes that make up the polygon, and whatever data values are stored with the polygon (temperature, stress, etc.). Consider the example of two polygons below.

**Figure 10.6**
*Two Polygons Example*

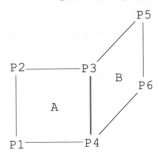

This example is similar to Figure 10.4 except that we have replaced the (X,Y,Z) values of the nodes with node names and have added an additional polygon called B. The node list for this example is shown below.

**Figure 10.7**
*Node List for Figure 10.6*

| Node Name | X | Y | Z |
|-----------|---|---|---|
| P1 | 0 | 0 | 0 |
| P2 | 0 | 1 | 0 |
| P3 | 1 | 1 | 0 |
| P4 | 1 | 0 | 0 |
| P5 | 1 | 1 | 1 |
| P6 | 1 | 0 | 1 |

Here is the polygon list for the same example.

**Figure 10.8**
*Polygon List for Figure 10.6*

| Polygon Name | Nodes | Nearest Neighbors | Temperature | Stress |
|--------------|-------|-------------------|-------------|--------|
| A | P1,P2,P3,P4 | B | 34.7 | .023 |
| B | P4,P3,P5,P6 | A | 23.1 | .028 |

Why bother having a separate node list? Why not just list the (X, Y, Z) locations of the nodes that make up a particular polygon? The reason is that most nodes are used by several different polygons. In the example above, nodes P3 and P4 are used by both polygon A and polygon B.

*Polygonal datasets contain node lists and polygon lists.*

In this example there are two data values (temperature and stress) stored with each polygon. Typically there are several data values per polygon.

Sometimes, each polygon has its own (X, Y, Z) position, in addition to the node locations. In that case, all of the node coordinates are relative to these polygon locations. We will ignore this possible complication in this chapter.

## A Cube Example

We continue with a somewhat more complex example. Figure 10.9 shows two perspective views of a cube: one from the upper right, and another from the lower left.

**Figure 10.9**
*Two Views of a Cube*

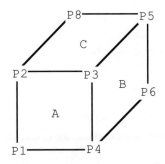
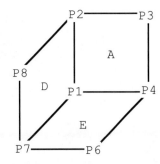

Given these two views, all the nodes and all the polygons except one are visible. The polygon at the rear of the cube (F) is not visible in either view. Here is the node list for this cube.

**Figure 10.10**
*Node List for Figure 10.9*

| Node Name | X | Y | Z |
|---|---|---|---|
| P1 | 0 | 0 | 0 |
| P2 | 0 | 1 | 0 |
| P3 | 1 | 1 | 0 |
| P4 | 1 | 0 | 0 |
| P5 | 1 | 1 | 1 |
| P6 | 1 | 0 | 1 |
| P7 | 0 | 0 | 1 |
| P8 | 0 | 1 | 1 |

The polygon list for the cube is shown below.

**Figure 10.11**
*Polygon List for Figure 10.9*

| Polygon Name | Nodes | Nearest Neighbors | Temperature | Stress |
|---|---|---|---|---|
| A | P1,P2,P3,P4 | B,C,D,E | 34.7 | .023 |
| B | P4,P3,P5,P6 | A,C,E,F | 23.1 | .028 |
| C | P2,P3,P5,P8 | A,B,D,F | 24.5 | .024 |
| D | P1,P2,P7,P8 | A,C,E,F | 29.4 | .033 |
| E | P1,P4,P6,P7 | A,B,D,F | 28.6 | .023 |
| F | P5,P6,P7,P8 | B,C,D,E | 31.9 | .031 |

Even for this simple cube example, the bookkeeping gets to be a pain. Imagine what it is like for an actual problem with thousands of polygons! Deciding on and constructing the grid and these tables are major tasks of any polygonal data project. Thankfully, once you have constructed the grid, it is relatively easy to pull out the data and visualize it.

Note that although we have been using squares for our polygonal examples, triangles are probably more commonly used as the polygons for a polygonal dataset.

## Binary vs. ASCII Text

As mentioned before, all polygonal datasets are organized as columns. This means that the data could easily be stored as ASCII text numbers, except that polygonal datasets tend to be very large. Therefore, standard binary formats for polygonal data are becoming more popular—formats such as DXF, IGES, etc.

*CAD*=Computer Aided Design
For creating objects
on a computer.

*FEA*=Finite Element Analysis
For analyzing object behavior
on a computer.

However, some of these formats are more frequently used for defining *objects* for CAD (Computer Aided Design) programs than for defining *data*. The process of using polygonal data to simulate an object is often called Finite Element Analysis, or *FEA*.

## From Surfaces to Solids

In all of our examples, the main object was a polygon. These polygons were 2-dimensional surfaces, even though they were positioned in 3D. Sometimes, people will use a *solid* as the main object—for example, a cube. In this case, the data values would be defined at the center of the cube instead of the center of the polygon.

Everything with solids is the same as in our examples, but with the additional complication of the extra dimension.

## Visualizing Polygonal Data

As mentioned above, creating polygonal data is conceptually much more difficult than visualizing it. The most common way to visualize polygonal data is to position the polygons in 3D space and use color raster imaging to color each polygon according to its data value.

**Figure 10.12**
*A Cube with Gray Levels*
*Representing Temperature*

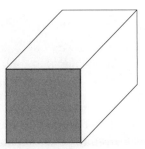

In the example above, the faces of the cube are colored according to the value of temperature on that face of the cube.

Complications can arise because many of the polygons may be hidden from view from a particular perspective. Therefore, as in volumetric visualization, wide use is made of animations, in order to bring hidden polygons into view.

## Polygonal to 3D Matrix

A more serious complication occurs when polygons are completely enclosed by other polygons. One solution to this problem is to selectively remove polygons for viewing the interior. Another way is to convert the data to a 3D matrix, and then use standard 3D matrix visualization tools to 'see inside.' See Chapter 11 for more information on the conversion of polygonal data to 3D matrix data.

In addition, it is common to have both polygonal data and 3D matrix data in the same project. An example would be air flowing around a wing. In this case you could use both 3D matrix technology (perhaps with a warped grid) to model the airflow around the wing, and polygonal technology to model the wing itself.

In such a case, you might want to see data from both sides in the same view. The commercial programs that show both types of data simultaneously are currently very expensive—though hopefully that will change. In the meantime, some people convert the polygonal data to 3D matrix data, embed it in the proper location of the larger 3D matrix dataset, and visualize everything with a low-cost 3D matrix visualization program.

### Photorealistic Rendering

A huge amount of time and effort is spent making computers render 3D scenes that look like photographs—such that there is a vast array of hardware and software for 3D rendering.

We mention this because often the 3D objects in these scenes are defined by polygons. Therefore, this large technology base can be used to produce photorealistic rendering not only of created scenes, but of polygonal datasets!

Photorealistic rendering technology can smooth over the borders between polygons, add highlights from computer-generated light sources, add shadows, add reflections, and otherwise enhance images.

It is not clear whether photorealistic rendering helps people gain additional insight into their data, and it requires huge amounts of computer power. Where the techniques are most useful is in presentation of your data to a wide audience. The photorealistic techniques can make it easier for people to see the three dimensionality of the data.

## Summary

In this chapter we have discussed the organization of polygonal data, concentrating on how nodes and nearest neighbors are defined and stored. We have also talked briefly about how polygonal datasets are visualized.

# CHAPTER 11
# CONVERSIONS & ADDING DIMENSIONS

## Overview

In this chapter we describe conversions from one type of data organization to another. The most common and important conversion is from column data to 2D matrix or 3D matrix data. We describe this conversion process in detail. We also discuss how adding dimensions to your data can help you analyze and visualize it.

By using the conversion methods described here, you can perform powerful 2D matrix and 3D matrix visualization and analysis, even for data that does not fit on a structured grid.

We also describe conversions from polygonal data to matrix data, from 2D matrix to 3D matrix data (and vice versa), and from 1D column to 2D matrix data.

## Column Data to 2D Matrix Data

We have described the conversion of column data to matrix data when the data falls on a uniform or even a warped grid. But what happens if the data locations have no particular pattern?

In that case, you need to use one of the methods described here to convert your column data to matrix data. It is often very useful to do this conversion, because of the powerful matrix analysis and visualization tools available.

*Steps to Convert*
*Scatter Data to Matrix Data*
**Step 1**: *Grid the scatter data*
**Step 2**: *Fill missing values*

Column data that is 2-dimensional or 3-dimensional but does not fall on a uniform grid is called *scatter data*. The conversion of scatter data to matrix data happens in two steps. In this first step, the scatter data is *gridded*, or placed into a grid based on the data locations for every data value. In the second step, the *missing data values* of that matrix are filled. Each of these steps is described below.

## Step 1: Gridding Scatter Data

The first step in the process of converting column scatter data to matrix data is to place the data values into a grid. Any time you grid data, you have to make a choices about the destination grid (such as grid size). This section should help you make intelligent choices.

We start with the following column dataset example.

**Figure 11.1**
*Column Data Example
of Scatter Data*

| X | Y | Velocity |
|---|---|----------|
| 0.3 | 0.3 | 0.0350 |
| 0.7 | 1.0 | 0.0714 |
| 0.5 | 1.5 | 0.3853 |
| 1.1 | 0.8 | 0.4911 |
| 1.0 | 1.0 | 0.2422 |
| 1.0 | 1.2 | 0.9207 |
| 1.5 | 0.5 | 0.5744 |
| 1.3 | 1.0 | 0.3305 |
| 1.5 | 1.5 | 0.8485 |

The scatter plot of this dataset is shown in Figure 11.2. We have labeled each point with the data value corresponding to that point. Note that in this scatter plot, the Y values increase *downward*.

**Figure 11.2**
*Plot of Scatter Data Example*

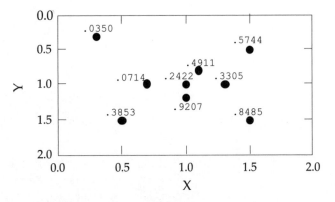

We now *grid* the data (also called *binning* the data) by first creating a grid, and then using the data locations to decide where to put each data value into the grid.

## A 3 × 3 Grid Example

We select a 3 × 3 destination grid (shown in Figure 11.3). The data locations on the destination grid were chosen to go from the X and Y minimum location values (0.3,0.3) to the X and Y maximum location values (1.5,1.5) in constant increments (0.6 in both X and Y).

**Figure 11.3**
*Blank 3×3 2D Matrix*

| | | X | | |
|---|---|---|---|---|
| | | 0.3 | 0.9 | 1.5 |
| | 0.3 | | | |
| Y | 0.9 | | | |
| | 1.5 | | | |

We overlay this proposed grid onto the scatter plot as shown in Figure 11.4 below. The labels for the grid X and Y location values are on the top and right of the graph. Note again, Y values increase *downward* when we show a scatter plot. (We flipped the axis for graphs in this chapter to make it easy to compare the scatter plot to the matrices.)

**Figure 11.4**
*Scatter Plot Example with 3×3 Grid*

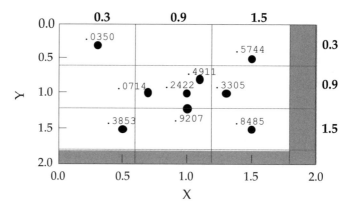

Note that each grid (X, Y) pair defines a *box*, not a *point*. This is because each grid pair is considered a label for a *range* of data locations. The range for each (X,Y) data location is shown by the gray grid lines in Figure 11.4. .

For example, the grid location of (0.9,1.5) encompasses the range (0.6<X<1.2, 1.2<Y<1.8). The shaded boxes on the graph are regions that are not covered by the grid defined by Figure 11.3.

The range of an X or Y data location on the grid is defined as going from halfway to its neighbor on the left (or bottom) to halfway to its neighbor on the right (or top).

For grid data locations at the edge of the matrix, the range is chosen so it is symmetrical left and right (or up and down). For example, in Figure 11.4 the X data location of 1.5 extends to the left down to 1.2, which is 0.3 away from 1.5. We therefore extend the data location 0.3 to the right, which is 1.5+0.3=1.8.

Each of these boxes for each (X,Y) data location pair is called a *bin* (hence the alternate term of *binning* for the gridding of data). The data values are placed into their appropriate bins in the matrix as follows.

**Figure 11.5**
*3×3 2D Matrix with Gridded Scatter Data*

|   |     | X |  |  |
|---|-----|--------|--------|--------|
|   |     | **0.3** | **0.9** | **1.5** |
|   | **0.3** | 0.0350 | NaN | 0.5744 |
| **Y** | **0.9** | NaN | 0.2682 | 0.3305 |
|   | **1.5** | 0.3853 | 0.9207 | 0.8485 |

Note that there are two NaNs in the matrix, because there are no data values with data locations inside the (0.9,0.3) and (0.3,0.9) bins. You can see this clearly in Figure 11.4.

Note also that the value at (0.9,0.9) does not correspond to any data value in Figure 11.1. This is because three of the data values were inside this particular bin. These three data values (0.4911,0.2422,0.0714) were averaged to produce the data value (0.2682) that you see for that bin.

By the way, there are other ways to deal with multiple values in a bin: some people like to have only the latest value in the bin, not an average of all the values in the bin.

Look also at the data value of 0.9207. In Figure 11.4 it is not clear whether that value should go into the (0.9,1.5) bin or the (0.9,0.9) bin. Since the original Y data location for that value was right on the dividing line between the two bins, which one it falls into depends on the details of the computational routine that does the binning.

## A 4 × 4 Grid Example

The size of the destination grid is completely arbitrary. It will be illuminating to grid the data again, but this time on a slightly larger, 4 × 4 grid. The new destination grid is shown in Figure 11.6.

**Figure 11.6**
*Blank 4×4 2D Matrix*

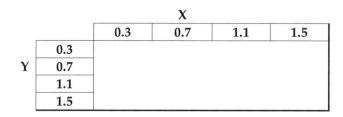

| | | X | | | |
|---|---|---|---|---|---|
| | | 0.3 | 0.7 | 1.1 | 1.5 |
| | 0.3 | | | | |
| Y | 0.7 | | | | |
| | 1.1 | | | | |
| | 1.5 | | | | |

The data locations on the destination grid were again chosen to span the X and Y minimum to maximum values in constant increments. Since there are now 4 bins per axis, the increment is now 0.4 instead of 0.6. A scatter plot of the data, with the bin boundaries overlaid, is shown below.

**Figure 11.7**
*Scatter Plot Example with 4×4 Grid*

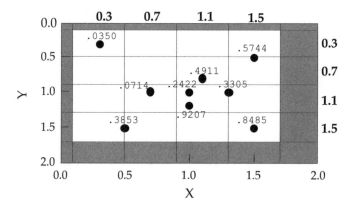

The gray areas in Figure 11.7 are somewhat larger than the gray areas in Figure 11.4. This is because as the grid gets bigger, the size of the bin for each (X,Y) pair gets smaller. In particular, the size of the bins at the edges of the grid (which have the same locations of 0.3 or 1.5 in Figures 11.4 and 11.7) are smaller here. Hence, the region not covered by the grid is somewhat bigger.

The data values are binned into the 4 × 4 destination grid as shown in Figure 11.8.

**Figure 11.8**
*4×4 2D Matrix with Gridded Scatter Data*

|   | X |   |   |   |
|---|---|---|---|---|
|   | **0.3** | **0.7** | **1.1** | **1.5** |
| **0.3** | 0.0350 | NaN | NaN | 0.5744 |
| **Y**   **0.7** | NaN | NaN | 0.4911 | NaN |
| **1.1** | NaN | 0.0714 | 0.4978 | NaN |
| **1.5** | 0.3853 | NaN | NaN | 0.8485 |

Both this matrix and the matrix shown in Figure 11.5 have bins that contain the average of multiple data values. In this case the bin at (1.1,1.1) is set to the average of the three values it contains (0.9207, 0.2422, and 0.3305).

As you make the destination grid bigger and bigger, however, the number of bins that contain multiple data values will decrease and eventually reach zero. This will happen when the grid increment is less than the smallest distance between two datapoints.

Note also that there are nine NaNs, as opposed to only two in Figure 11.5. This is to be expected, since there are only nine data values in the original dataset, but 16 bin locations in Figure 11.8. Therefore, there must be at least 16-9=7 NaNs in the resulting grid. The two 'extra' NaNs come from the fact that three data values all fell into the same bin.

## Selecting Destination Grid Size

What size should your destination grid be? The answer depends on balancing two conflicting demands. On the one hand, you want as big a grid as possible, because every time two data values fall into the same bin you lose information. But on the other hand, you want as small a grid as possible, to reduce the number of NaNs to a minimum.

### Reducing Bin Averaging

Once two data values are averaged to the same bin you have lost information on their different values and their different locations. In addition, the accuracy of the locations is now the size of the bin, not whatever accuracy you had originally for the data locations.

*For highest positional accuracy, grid increment ≤ smallest difference between two datapoints.*

Therefore, the best grid to reduce the averaging of data values is one that has an increment smaller than the smallest distance between two data values.

## Reducing Missing Values

Before a 2D matrix can be analyzed or visualized, the NaNs must be filled in with some values. We describe in detail below several ways to fill in these values. *All* of the methods, however, become less accurate as the number of NaNs increases. Therefore, for highest data value accuracy, it is best to keep the grid divided into as few data elements as possible.

*For highest data accuracy, grid size=square root of number of datapoints.*

If the datapoints are reasonably uniformly spaced, you will have only a few NaNs with a grid size in each direction equal to the square root of the total number of datapoints. With this choice, the number of bins is exactly equal to the number of datapoints, so for a completely uniformly spaced grid, the number of NaNs is zero.

A good rule of thumb is to use the square root rule for uniformly spaced data, but use the smallest difference rule if you have areas where the datapoint spacing is much tighter than in other areas.

## Missing Data Flags

We have used NaN in the discussion above to show grid locations that do not have a value. There are numerous other ways to code for what is often called *missing data*. For example, in Figures 8.18 and 8.19, the value 99999 was used to code for missing data. In Figure 5.33, the value -99.0 was used to code for missing data.

*Missing data code should be outside the allowed range of values.*

These values are used because not all computers support NaN. If you decide to use a numeric value to code for a missing value, make sure that the missing value number is outside the allowed range of values for the data. For example, -99 is lower than any possible outside temperature (at least in the continental United States), and 99999 is much larger than any valid intensity value for the image in Figure 8.20.

## Step 2: Filling Missing Data

The second step of the process of converting scatter data to matrix data is changing all the missing data elements to data values. There are dozens of methods for doing this. Some methods are simple, fast, and inaccurate; others are extremely computationally intensive and very sophisticated.

*Methods differ in how much they smooth the matrix data, whether they preserve known data values, and whether they contain discontinuities in the data values.*

The various methods also differ in how much they *smooth* the data. In particular, some methods smooth the resulting data matrix so much that the *known* data values are changed. For some of the simple methods, you must smooth the resulting data matrix after 'filling' to get rid of sharp discontinuities in the data. The most advanced methods try to preserve known data values and also try to avoid discontinuities in the matrix.

If you have only a few missing data elements, then any method will do. If, instead, you have a matrix with mostly missing data elements and only a few valid data values, then you should use the best method available to you.

We present here a small sample of the current methods, concentrating on the simplest methods and on the most sophisticated filling method, known as *kriging*.

### Nearest Neighbor Fill

The simplest method of filling missing data values is to set them to the closest valid number, called *nearest neighbor fill*. Consider the following sample dataset, extracted from a much larger matrix of **Dr. Wolfram Herth**'s groundwater dataset.

*Figure 11.9*
*Sample Dataset Extracted from Herth Groundwater Dataset*

|   |       | \| | \| | X | \| | \| |
|---|-------|--------|--------|--------|--------|--------|
|   |       | 27500  | 28000  | 28500  | 29000  | 29500  |
|   | 19595 | -15.91 | NaN    | -16.30 | NaN    | -16.68 |
|   | 19945 | NaN    | NaN    | NaN    | NaN    | NaN    |
| Y | 20295 | NaN    | NaN    | NaN    | NaN    | NaN    |
|   | 20645 | -14.15 | -14.37 | NaN    | NaN    | NaN    |
|   | 20995 | -13.36 | -13.57 | NaN    | NaN    | -13.96 |
|   | 21344 | NaN    | -12.56 | -12.75 | -12.89 | -12.98 |

A grayscale image of this dataset is shown in Figure 11.10. Note that black blocks are for the NaN cells.

**Figure 11.10**
*Grayscale Plot of*
*Groundwater Data*
*in Figure 11.9*

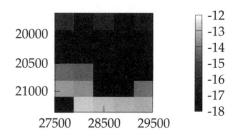

After a nearest neighbor fill, the dataset now looks like :

**Figure 11.11**
*Sample Dataset Filled with*
*Nearest Neighbor Routine*

|   |       | X |  |  |  |  |
|---|-------|-------|-------|-------|-------|-------|
|   |       | **27500** | **28000** | **28500** | **29000** | **29500** |
|   | **19595** | -15.91 | -15.91 | -16.30 | -16.30 | -16.68 |
|   | **19945** | -15.91 | -15.91 | -16.30 | -16.30 | -16.68 |
| **Y** | **20295** | -14.15 | -14.37 | -14.37 | -13.96 | -13.96 |
|   | **20645** | -14.15 | -14.37 | -14.37 | -13.96 | -13.96 |
|   | **20995** | -13.36 | -13.57 | -12.75 | -12.89 | -13.96 |
|   | **21344** | -13.36 | -12.56 | -12.75 | -12.89 | -12.98 |

Note that the missing data values have been filled with exact copies of their nearest neighbor values. This produces a very chunky matrix with many discontinuities, as can be seen below.

**Figure 11.12**
*Grayscale Plot of*
*Groundwater Data*
*in Figure 11.11*

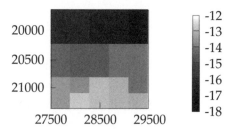

**Nearest Neighbor Fill**
*Very fast; works best if only a*
*few values are missing.*

Nearest neighbor filling only makes sense if you have just a few missing data values. It works wonderfully, for example, on **Dr. Mike Astroe**'s dataset, as seen in Figure 8.18. To people who insist on using this method for datasets with larger missing data regions, we strongly recommend a separate *smoothing pass* to get rid of the chunkiness.

## Linear Interpolation

One step up from nearest neighbor filling is the *linear interpolation* method of filling missing data values. In this method, the missing data values are interpolated from the closest data values in the same column, in the same row, or both.

### Linear Interpolation along Rows

Below is the matrix resulting from linearly interpolating along rows of the sample dataset.

|  |  | X | | | | |
|---|---|---|---|---|---|---|
|  |  | 27500 | 28000 | 28500 | 29000 | 29500 |
|  | 19595 | −15.91 | −16.10 | −16.30 | −16.49 | −16.68 |
|  | 19945 | NaN | NaN | NaN | NaN | NaN |
| Y | 20295 | NaN | NaN | NaN | NaN | NaN |
|  | 20645 | −14.15 | −14.37 | −14.59 | −14.80 | −15.02 |
|  | 20995 | −13.36 | −13.57 | −13.70 | −13.83 | −13.96 |
|  | 21344 | −12.37 | −12.56 | −12.75 | −12.89 | −12.98 |

The values in all rows, except the second and third, are interpolated between their neighbors in each row. There were no known data values in those rows, so they continue to be filled with NaNs.

**Figure 11.14**
*Grayscale Plot of Groundwater Data in Figure 11.13*

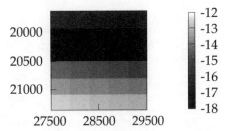

Linear interpolation *along rows* does not work well for this dataset, since there are streaks of NaNs in the result. Linear interpolation *along columns* is not much better: there will be no NaNs left, but there will still be streaks.

### Linear Interpolation along Columns and Rows

It is relatively common, however, to interpolate in two passes: first along columns, then using the resulting data to interpolate along rows. The interpolated dataset is shown below.

**Figure 11.15**
*Sample Dataset Filled with Linear Interpolation along Rows and Columns*

|   |       | X       |         |         |         |         |
|---|-------|---------|---------|---------|---------|---------|
|   |       | 27500   | 28000   | 28500   | 29000   | 29500   |
|   | 19595 | -15.91  | -16.44  | -16.30  | -14.69  | -16.68  |
|   | 19945 | -15.33  | -15.75  | -15.66  | -14.41  | -16.07  |
| Y | 20295 | -14.74  | -15.06  | -15.02  | -14.13  | -15.45  |
|   | 20645 | -14.15  | -14.37  | -14.38  | -13.85  | -14.83  |
|   | 20995 | -13.36  | -13.57  | -13.58  | -13.36  | -13.96  |
|   | 21344 | -12.47  | -12.56  | -12.75  | -12.89  | -12.98  |

We have eliminated all NaNs by adding the second pass. The resulting grayscale image looks like the following.

**Figure 11.16**
*Grayscale Plot of Groundwater Data in Figure 11.15*

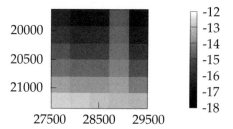

You should be able to see *streaks*, even in this small sample. This is the major disadvantage of the linear interpolation method of filling missing data: it produces streaks because in each pass information only from data in a particular row or column is used to set the values in that row or column.

**Linear Interpolation**
*Fast but produces streaks. Best when you do not want to average values between rows (or columns) but do want to average between columns (or rows).*

Linear interpolation is useful when you do not want any mixing of data between rows or columns. Consider, for example, a 2D matrix of US population values by state, where the Y axis is the state and the X axis is the year. It may make sense to linearly interpolate the population values from other years for a particular state (along rows), but it would make no sense to interpolate from other states (along columns). To fill missing values in that case, linear interpolation along rows is the *only* method that makes sense.

## Smooth Fill

One interpolation method that does not produce streaks is known as a *smooth fill*. In this procedure, each missing data element is set to the average of its eight immediate neighbors. An example of a missing value (in the center) and its neighbors is shown below.

**Figure 11.17**
*Smoothed Fill Example*

| 1 | 2 | NaN |
|---|-----|-----|
| 3 | NaN | 4 |
| 5 | NaN | 6 |

For example, a smooth fill pass would set the center NaN in Figure 11.17 above to the following value:

**Figure 11.18**
*Calculation of NaN using Smooth Fill*

$$[\ ] = \frac{(1+2+3+4+5+6)}{6} = 3.5$$

Note that only the six known data values are averaged in this example: the NaN entries are treated as if they were not there. Figure 11.19 shows the results of a single, smooth fill pass on the example dataset from Figure 11.9.

**Figure 11.19**
*Sample Dataset after Single Smooth Fill Pass*

|   |       | X |  |  |  |  |
|---|-------|--------|--------|--------|--------|--------|
|   |       | 27500 | 28000 | 28500 | 29000 | 29500 |
|   | 19595 | -15.91 | -16.11 | -16.30 | -16.49 | -16.68 |
|   | 19945 | -15.91 | -16.11 | -16.30 | -16.49 | -16.68 |
| Y | 20295 | -14.26 | -14.26 | -14.37 | NaN | NaN |
|   | 20645 | -13.86 | -13.86 | -13.97 | -13.96 | -13.96 |
|   | 20995 | -13.60 | -13.46 | -13.22 | -13.14 | -13.28 |
|   | 21344 | -13.16 | -13.06 | -12.94 | -13.14 | -13.28 |

Note that the data elements at (29000,20295) and (29500,20295) are still set to NaN. That is because those data locations did not have any neighbors. Because of this problem, most smooth fill routines do multiple passes until there are no NaNs left.

Note that in Figure 11.19 the known data values have been modified (compare to Figure 11.9). This is because the smoothed fill routine works not only on missing data values, but also on known data values. For example, in Figure 11.20 the data value in the center is equal to 3.5.

**Figure 11.20**
*Another Smoothed
Fill Example*

| 1 | 2 | 3 |
|---|-----|---|
| 3 | 3.5 | 4 |
| 5 | 4.5 | 6 |

However, after a smooth fill pass, it is equal to the following:

**Figure 11.21**
*Calculation of a Data Value
Using Smoothed Fill*

$$[\ ] = \frac{(1+2+3+3+3.5+4+5+4.5+6)}{9} = 3.55$$

Clearly, this method smoothes the data very heavily. If there are large NaN regions so the routine has to do several passes, the 2D matrix can smooth away to an almost uniform value.

The sample dataset after two smooth fill passes is shown below.

**Figure 11.22**
*Sample Dataset
after Two
Smooth Fill Passes*

|  |  | X | | | | |
|---|---|---|---|---|---|---|
|  |  | 27500 | 28000 | 28500 | 29000 | 29500 |
|  | 19595 | −15.98 | −16.10 | −16.30 | −16.49 | −16.62 |
|  | 19945 | −15.40 | −15.50 | −15.80 | −16.19 | −16.62 |
| Y | 20295 | −14.68 | −14.76 | −14.91 | −15.10 | −15.29 |
|  | 20645 | −13.88 | −13.87 | −13.78 | −13.71 | −13.63 |
|  | 20995 | −13.48 | −13.43 | −13.38 | −13.41 | −13.47 |
|  | 21344 | −13.21 | −13.12 | −13.05 | −13.10 | −13.19 |

The corresponding grayscale image is shown below.

**Figure 11.23**
*Grayscale Plot of
Groundwater Data
in Figure 11.22*

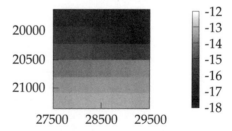

**Smooth Fill**
*Fast, but produces heavily
smoothed dataset.*

Smoothed fill is best used when you want a highly smoothed dataset, or when there are only a few missing data values.

## Weighted Fill

The *weighted fill* routine is similar to the smoothed fill routine, but with a twist. In smoothed fill, the missing data element is set to the average of the element's nearest neighbors. In weighted fill, the missing data element is set to the *weighted* average of a much larger *region* surrounding the missing data element. Known data values that are close to the missing data element are weighed heavily, while those far away are not weighed much at all.

**Figure 11.24**
*Groundwater Data with Weighting Circles*

|   | | 27500 | 28000 | 28500 | 29000 | 29500 |
|---|---|---|---|---|---|---|
| | 19595 | -15.91 | NaN | -16.30 | NaN | -16.68 |
| | 19945 | NaN | NaN | NaN | NaN | NaN |
| Y | 20295 | NaN | NaN | NaN | N A | B C |
| | 20645 | -14.15 | -14.37 | NaN | NaN | NaN |
| | 20995 | -13.36 | -13.57 | NaN | NaN | -13.96 |
| | 21344 | NaN | -12.56 | -12.75 | -12.89 | -12.98 |

In Figure 11.24 above, the boxed missing data element is surrounded with three regions[*], A, B, and C, of increasing distance from that element.

Data values that are closer to the boxed missing data element are weighed more heavily. For example, inside the region marked A there is one known data value, -14.37. This value will be arbitrarily assigned a weighting of 1.0.

Inside the region marked B there are two more data values, -13.57 and -16.30. These values will be given a weighting of 0.6.

**Figure 11.25**
*Calculation of NaN using Weighted Fill*

Inside the region marked C, there are four more data values: -14.15, -12.56, -12.75, and -12.89. These values each will be given a weighting of 0.1. The boxed missing data element is therefore set to the following:

$$[\ ] = \frac{1.0 \times (-14.37) + 0.6 \times (-13.57 - 16.30) + 0.1 \times (-14.15 - 12.56 - 12.75 - 12.89)}{1.0 + 2 \times 0.6 + 4 \times 0.1} = 14.43$$

[*] The elipses would be circles except the data values in this figure are spaced much farther apart in one direction than in the other.

You might even consider the smoothing fill routine as a limiting case of the weighted fill routine, where there is only one region: its radius is 1 data element, its weighting factor, 1.

*Weighted fill routine requires a weighting factor function and a cutoff radius.*

The weighted fill routine requires two parameters: the *weighting factors* as a function of radius, and a *cutoff radius*. In the example above, we chose a cutoff radius of around 2.0 (in units of data elements) and arbitrarily picked weighting factors.

### Weighted Factor Functions

In most weighted fill routines, the weighting factors come from evaluating a user-supplied function of radius. Three common weighting factor functions are given in Figure 11.26.

**Figure 11.26**
*Three Common Weighting Factor Functions*

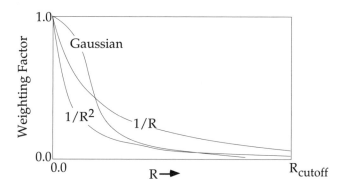

Which function you use depends on the data. The $1/R$ and $1/R^2$ functions weigh close values most heavily, and hence do not smooth the values much. The Gaussian function will smooth moderately, since it weighs values farther away more heavily. However, the Gaussian function does drop off more rapidly at large radii.

### Cutoff Radius

Weighted fill routines use a cutoff radius, so the computer does not spend an inordinate amount of time weighing values that are so distant they have a negligible effect on the current location.

*It is best to choose the cutoff radius on the basis of number of datapoints enclosed by cutoff circle.*

The cutoff radius is usually calculated so it encompasses a fixed number of known data values. For example, if there were no missing data values, the number of data values $N$ would be

$$N=\pi R^2$$

where, again, R is measured in data element units. If only a certain fraction f of the matrix locations contain known data values (the rest being *missing* values), then

$$N = f\pi R^2 .$$

So a good choice for cutoff radius $R_{cutoff}$ to keep N data values inside that radius is

**Figure 11.27**
*Calculation of $R_{cutoff}$*

$$R_{cutoff} = \sqrt{\frac{N}{f\pi}} .$$

Setting N=20 and f=.5 gives a cutoff radius $R_{cutoff}$ = 3.65.

By the way, note that we have defined the cutoff radius in units of data elements, which makes sense if the X axis spacing is the same as the Y axis spacing. If these spacings are not equal, then it is better to use the radius in terms of the X and Y distance scales. That way, the known data will influence the missing data element based on its closeness in terms of data locations, not in terms of matrix locations.

## Secondary Passes

The weighted fill routine is usually a single pass routine. However, data locations farther away than $R_{cutoff}$ from a known data value will *not* be filled. Some routines will leave these NaNs and expect you to perform a second pass, increase the cutoff radius, or fill them with another method such as smooth fill.

In any case, the results of running a weighted fill routine with a Gaussian weighting factor function and a cutoff radius of 2 on the example dataset are shown below.

**Figure 11.28**
*Sample Dataset
After Weighted Fill
(Gaussian)*

|   |       | X |       |       |       |       |
|---|-------|--------|--------|--------|--------|--------|
|   |       | 27500  | 28000  | 28500  | 29000  | 29500  |
|   | 19595 | -15.86 | -16.02 | -16.27 | -16.49 | -16.67 |
|   | 19945 | -15.33 | -15.42 | -16.01 | -16.40 | -16.56 |
| Y | 20295 | -14.29 | -14.31 | -14.71 | -15.08 | -15.12 |
|   | 20645 | -13.87 | -13.85 | -13.68 | -13.50 | -13.74 |
|   | 20995 | -13.60 | -13.47 | -13.19 | -13.18 | -13.45 |
|   | 21344 | -13.32 | -13.12 | -12.94 | -13.03 | -13.27 |

Comparing this matrix to that in Figure 11.9, it is clear that the known data values have not been preserved (as was also the case in the smooth fill routine). In fact, there is little difference between this dataset and the one shown in Figure 11.22 for the smooth fill routine. This can be verified if you compare the grayscale image of this dataset (Figure 11.29) with the image shown in Figure 11.23.

**Figure 11.29**
*Grayscale Plot of
Groundwater Data
in Figure 11.28*

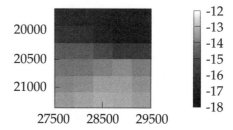

To the eye they are virtually identical. One reason for this is our use of the *Gaussian* weighting factor function, which produces a moderate amount of smoothing. Another reason is that, in this example, every missing data value is—at most—only two data elements away from a known data value.

The differences between the routines only become obvious when you have large missing value areas. In that case, the weighted fill routine is more accurate and will produce many fewer artifacts in the resulting dataset.

### Comparing Weighted Fill and Smooth Fill

To see the differences between weighted fill and smooth fill, we go back to **Wolfram Herth**'s full dataset. A grayscale scatter plot of the whole dataset is shown in Figure 11.30. Black areas are the missing data regions.

**Figure 11.30**
Grayscale Image of
Herth Dataset

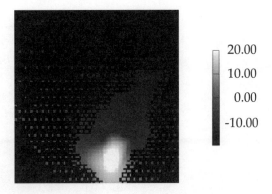

This dataset is a good test of these routines because it includes
regions of very dense known data values, *and* areas where known
data values are very sparse. A good routine can handle both
extremes. The results of a smooth fill and of a weighted fill with a
$1/R^2$ function and a cutoff radius of 4 are shown below.

**Figure 11.31**
Grayscale Image of Smooth
Filled and Weighted Filled
Herth Groundwater Dataset

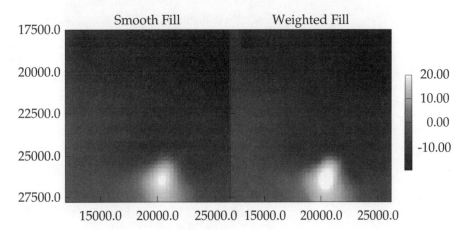

It is probably difficult to pick out the differences from this printed
grayscale image (it is easier in color). So in Figure 11.32 we show as
a grayscale image the *difference* between the smooth fill dataset
and the weighted fill dataset.

**Figure 11.32**
*Difference between Smooth
Fill and Weighted Fill
Versions of Herth
Groundwater Dataset*

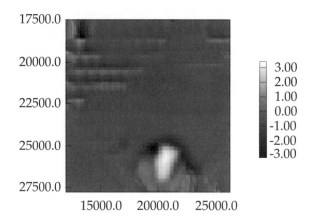

Here (finally) you can see the problems with the smooth fill. Note, first of all, the detail in the upper left of the 'difference' image. This difference exists because the weighted fill routine tried to keep a lot of the fine detail, and the smooth fill routine just smoothed it over, which is not always beneficial.

A much more serious problem is on the peak in the groundwater level, seen in the lower middle. In the original dataset this peak has virtually no missing data values and a maximum value around 24. The weighted fill routine maintained this maximum value, but the smooth fill routine brought the peak down to 21. This can be seen by noting on the color scale for Figure 11.32 that white corresponds to a difference of 3.0 between the weighted fill and smooth fill.

Note also the dark area around the peak on the difference image. This dark area appears because, in both the weighted fill dataset and the original dataset, the groundwater level has a very steep dropoff. In the smooth fill dataset, however, this steep dropoff is smoothed out, meaning that although in the smooth fill dataset the peak value *is less* than the original, the values around the peak *are more* than the original.

**Weighted Fill**
*Not very computationally
expensive, Good overall
routine, requires input of
weighting function and cutoff
radius.*

## Weighted Fill: Pros and Cons

The weighted fill routine is, for many datasets, a good compromise between computational complexity and time on the one hand, and the accuracy of the resulting matrix, on the other hand.

However, having to input the weighting function and the cutoff radius into the weighted fill routine is a problem: most users have no basis for choosing one function over another. Another problem with weighted fill can be seen in the example above. In the regions of few known data values, you would want a *large* cutoff radius and a *broad* weighting function. In the region near the peak with lots of known data values, you would want a *small* cutoff radius, and a very *narrow* weighting function.

## Kriging

What the world needs is a weighted fill method that automatically calculates the 'best' weighting function and cutoff radius at every point. This ideal routine would *know* where in the matrix to have a broad weighting function, and where to have a narrow one, and would adjust accordingly.

*Kriging comes from D. G. Krige, a South African engineer*

Such an algorithm exists! *Kriging*, (pronounced 'kreeging') is named after a South African engineer, D. G. Krige, who first developed the method. A complete description of the routine is beyond the scope of this book, but a conceptual outline of the technique is given below.

### Variances

In the language of kriging, every known data value and every missing data value has a *variance* associated with it. The variance is just a measure of the uncertainty of a value.[*] If you know a value exactly, its variance is *zero*. If you place absolutely no faith in a value, its variance is *one* (on a normalized scale).

The variance conceptually plays the same role in kriging as the weighting function plays in the weighted fill routine. For example, suppose you have a single known data value that you have assigned a variance of zero (you know it perfectly).

Since you have only one known value, all missing data locations must be assigned that value. You would be pretty sure the values that are close physically to that known value location would also be close numerically to the known value. With the values far away

---

[*] Mathematically, the variance is the square of the standard deviation.

physically, you would be a lot less sure of its value. This uncertainty is quantified below.

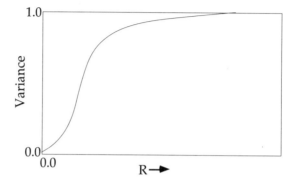

Figure 11.33 shows the variance curve for a single datapoint. Values near the known datapoint are certain (low variance); values far away are uncertain (high variance).

*Variance for a known data value should be set to the uncertainty of that value (most routines will set it to zero if the uncertainty is unknown).*

Note that the variance curve does *not* have to start from zero. If you happen to know how uncertain the known data value is (you could only measure height to the nearest inch, for example), then you could input that information into the variance for that data value.

## Creating the Variance Matrix

The variance curve looks like a weighting function curve, except that the vertical axis is flipped. And in fact, it is used like one. The next step in the kriging process is to estimate the missing data values, using these variance curves exactly as we used the weighting function curves in the weighted fill routine.

But now the techniques start to differ, because in addition to estimating the missing data *values*, the routine also estimates the *variance* at every missing data location. For example, a missing data location would have a low variance if it were surrounded by known values, but a high variance if it were far away from known values.

The result is the creation of a *variance matrix*, the same size as the data matrix. The variance matrix keeps track of the variances not only of the missing data value variances, but also of the known data value variances (which are either user-supplied or set to zero).

We will return to one vital point about this matrix: *the variances for the missing data values depend on the form of the variance curves chosen for each known data value.*

### Minimizing the Variance Matrix

The most important step in the kriging process is the one in which the variance matrix is minimized. Kriging tries to reduce the sum of all of the variances as much as possible by manipulating the variance curves associated with each known data value.

*Kriging is a lot like FFTs, in that nobody understands how either routine works, but they both perform magic and everybody uses them.*

At the end of this minimization process, every known data value will have a different variance curve. Because the variance curves change, not only will the *variance matrix* change, but the *data matrix* also will change. After kriging, the filled matrix contains the best possible estimate of the missing data values, in the sense that the variance has been minimized.

*Kriging is statistically the best possible fill routine.*

The minimization routine is complex and extremely computationally intensive. In particular, the number of calculations involved varies as $N^3$, where $N$ is the number of known data values. A straightforward kriging is therefore impractical on desktop computers for more than, say, 100 known data values. However, we describe below some ways around this limitation.

The minimization calculations involve a matrix inversion. This inversion can cause problems for the unwary. In particular, if two known (different) data values have the same data locations, the matrix inversion is *not defined*. (Most routines avoid this problem by scanning the data first and discarding duplicate locations.) The problem of an undefined matrix inversion does not occur in the examples described here, where we *bin* and *average* the data *first*.

*Kriging preserves known data values.*

Unlike smooth fill and weighted fill, kriging *preserves known data values*. It does this because the variance of the known values is fixed (usually at zero), so the minimization routine never has a chance to change either the variance or the corresponding data values.

## Co-linear Points

When the variance matrix is being minimized, a check is made for *co-linear* known datapoints. If known datapoints are co-linear with respect to the missing data value, the one farthest from the missing data location is given a very low weighting factor. Consider a sample matrix.

**Figure 11.34**
*Sample Dataset Extracted from Herth Groundwater Dataset*

| | | X | | | | |
|---|---|---|---|---|---|---|
| | | 27500 | 28000 | 28500 | 29000 | 29500 |
| | 19595 | -15.91 | NaN | -16.30 | NaN | -16.68 |
| | 19945 | NaN | NaN | NaN | NaN | NaN |
| Y | 20295 | NaN | NaN | NaN | NaN | NaN |
| | 20645 | -14.15 | -14.37 | NaN | NaN | NaN |
| | 20995 | -13.36 | -13.57 | NaN | NaN | -13.96 |
| | 21344 | NaN | -12.56 | -12.75 | -12.89 | -12.98 |

In the boxed NaN in the example above, the value of -14.37 has a very *strong* influence on the missing value, the value of -16.30 has a *small* influence on the missing value, and the value of -14.15 has *no* influence on the missing value.

Why does the -14.15 value have no influence? It is closer than the -16.30, which has *some* influence. The reason is that it is co-linear, or in a straight line, with the missing data location and a closer value (-14.37). The -14.15 value is *shadowed* by the closer value.

For example, consider if you had three height and distance measurements, all in a line, named A, B, and C. These three points are plotted below on a height-distance scatter plot.

**Figure 11.35**
*Three Points on a Height-Distance Plot*

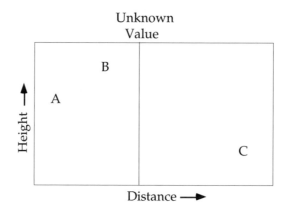

We want an estimate of the *height*, at the *distance* marked with a vertical line above. What is the best estimate of height? In the next figure we plot two lines on the graph. The points where those lines intersect the vertical line give us the height estimates.

**Figure 11.36**
*Two Fits to the Three Lines*

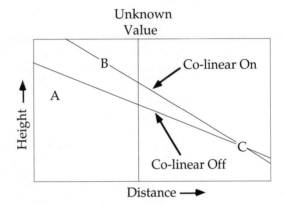

The *co-linear on* line defines an estimate of the height between B and C, ignoring the influence of A. The *co-linear off* line defines an estimate of the height between B and C, taking into account the influence of A.

If you think of A, B, and C defining a profile of a hill, it is clear that the best estimate of the unknown value is given by the *co-linear on* curve. A is on the other side of the peak marked by B.

Another way to think of it is that a missing data value is influenced by lots of known values, but primarily by the *closest* known value in any particular direction. This, in fact, is kriging's version of a cutoff radius, albeit one that varies not only for every missing data value, but also for every direction for each value!

## Subdividing the Region

It is possible to use kriging for datasets with more than 100 known data values, by using a trick.

The trick is to subdivide the matrix into a series of smaller subregions[*] which are kriged individually, then combined. The regions are chosen to overlap, so there are no obvious seams.

The subregioning may be done manually, or it may be done automatically by the computer. If the computer does the subregioning, it usually tries to keep about 50 known data values within a subregion.

How much does this help? Well, consider dividing $N$ known data values into $x$ subregions. Each subregion will have, on the average, $N/x$ known data values. The number of computations done in each subregion is proportional to the cube of the known values in that subregion, or $(N/x)^3$.

But there are $x$ subregions, so the total computational burden is $=x \times (N/x)^3$, or $N^3/x^2$. Therefore, creating $x$ subregions means that the number of calculations decreases by the factor $(1/x)^2$. So if you use 10 subregions, you can decrease your computer usage by a factor of 100!

## A Small Kriging Example

We return to the small example dataset from Figure 11.9. Below is that dataset after kriging.

Figure 11.37
Herth Groundwater
Dataset after Kriging

|   |       | X |||||
|---|-------|--------|--------|--------|--------|--------|
|   |       | 27500 | 28000 | 28500 | 29000 | 29500 |
|   | 19595 | -15.91 | -16.06 | -16.30 | -16.43 | -16.68 |
|   | 19945 | -15.39 | -15.58 | -15.76 | -15.91 | -16.03 |
| Y | 20295 | -14.81 | -15.00 | -15.10 | -15.23 | -15.34 |
|   | 20645 | -14.15 | -14.37 | -14.35 | -14.46 | -14.64 |
|   | 20995 | -13.36 | -13.57 | -13.52 | -13.65 | -13.96 |
|   | 21344 | -12.87 | -12.56 | -12.75 | -12.89 | -12.98 |

Note that the known data values have been preserved. The grayscale image of this dataset is shown below.

_____

[*] Samples are taken from subregions to estimate unknown values.

**Figure 11.38**
*Grayscale Plot of*
*Groundwater Data*
*in Figure 11.37*

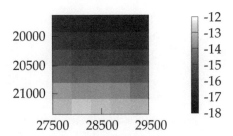

Kriging is the first example given in this chapter of a routine that produces such a smooth dataset *and* preserves known data values. This is one of its great strengths.

Below is the variance matrix for this dataset.

**Figure 11.39**
*Variance Matrix for*
*Herth Dataset*

|   |       | \multicolumn{5}{c}{X} |
|---|-------|-------|-------|-------|-------|-------|
|   |       | 27500 | 28000 | 28500 | 29000 | 29500 |
|   | 19595 | 0.00  | 0.07  | 0.00  | 0.08  | 0.00  |
|   | 19945 | 0.07  | 0.09  | 0.09  | 0.10  | 0.08  |
| Y | 20295 | 0.07  | 0.08  | 0.11  | 0.12  | 0.11  |
|   | 20645 | 0.00  | 0.00  | 0.10  | 0.11  | 0.08  |
|   | 20995 | 0.00  | 0.00  | 0.07  | 0.08  | 0.00  |
|   | 21344 | 0.05  | 0.00  | 0.00  | 0.00  | 0.00  |

The known data values all have variances of zero (we put those in). Note also that none of the variances gets very large, because there are no regions far away from known values. A grayscale image of the variance is shown below.

**Figure 11.40**
*Grayscale Plot of Variance*
*Matrix in Figure 11.39*

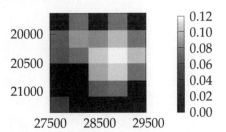

The black boxes correspond to the known data values. The white boxes are where the variance is the highest. As you would expect, the variance is highest for those locations farthest from known data values.

This sample dataset contains 12 known data values, was not subdivided, and took $0.02$ seconds to calculate on a Macintosh Quadra 700.

## A Larger Kriging Example

Here we take the entire Herth dataset, as shown in Figure 11.30, and krig it. The resulting image is shown in Figure 11.41.

**Figure 11.41**
*Grayscale Image of Kriged Herth Groundwater Dataset*

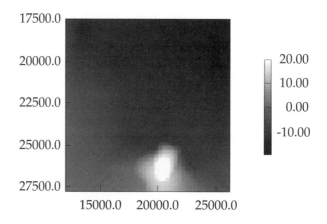

A grayscale plot of the variance matrix is shown below.

**Figure 11.42**
*Grayscale Image of Variance Matrix of Herth Groundwater Dataset*

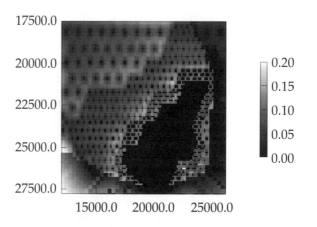

The black areas are where there were known data values. As expected, the areas with the highest variances are the ones farthest away from known data values.

So how does the kriged matrix compare to the matrices created with the smooth fill and weighted fill routines? A grayscale plot of the differences of the krig matrix and those two datasets is shown below.

**Figure 11.43**
*Grayscale Image of Differences between Krig Matrix and Smooth Fill and Weighted Fill Matrices*

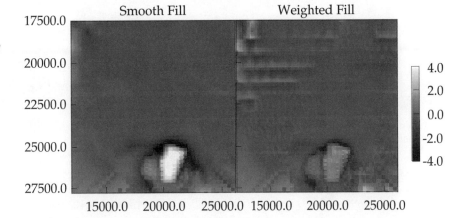

Once again, it is clear that the smooth fill routine handles the peak in the bottom middle of the dataset very poorly. It is off by as much as 20 percent in those regions. The weighted fill routine handles the peak much better (relative to kriging), but there are still some inaccuracies in the upper right.

This sample dataset contains 1,812 known data values, was subdivided extensively, and even with subdividing took 16 minutes to calculate on a Macintosh Quadra. If it were not for subdividing, the routine would still be grinding along into sometime next year.

## Kriging Summary

Clearly, kriging is superior to any other method discussed in this chapter for filling missing data values. It is also the only method that makes use of uncertainty values for your known data values. If you have fewer than 100 points on a large domain, it may be the only choice for the creation of a reasonably accurate matrix.

**Kriging**
*Guaranteed to be the most accurate, it will make use of uncertainties. But it extracts an extremely heavy computational toll.*

But of course the downside is the computational burden. Is it worth it? Not if you have only a few missing data values. And not if your known data values are fairly uniformly spaced. But if your data is as non-uniformly spaced as in the Herth example, kriging is highly recommended.

## Other Conversions

All conversions other than from column data to matrix data are pretty straightforward. They are listed here for reference.

### Column Data to 3D Matrix Data

We have explained in detail the process of converting column data to 2D matrix data. No mention was made of the conversion of column data to 3D matrix data. The reason is that every method carries over identically to three dimensions. The gridding process is identical, but of course with an extra dimension. And all of the missing data fill routines carry over trivially to three dimensions; even kriging can easily be made 3-dimensional.

### Polygonal Data to Matrix Data

The quickest way to convert polygonal data to matrix data is to first create a column dataset from the polygonal dataset. The columns will consist first of the $X$, $Y$, $Z$ data locations of the centers of all of the polygons (or the nodes for node-based datasets). Additional columns will contain the actual data values of those polygons.

Once this column dataset is created, then you can use all of the conversion technology described above.

### Matrix Data to Column Data

Creating column datasets from matrix datasets is easy, since a matrix is simply a more compact and efficient way of storing column data. Just create columns for the $X$, $Y$ or $X$, $Y$, $Z$ data locations, and additional columns for the data values. Then copy them out one by one.

A more interesting case occurs when you want to randomly sample the matrix. A randomly chosen data location typically will not correspond to a matrix data location. If so, to read a data value it is best to *interpolate* between the nearest data values in the matrix, as opposed to just using the nearest data value.

### 2D Matrix to 3D Matrix

It is often illuminating to consider a 2D matrix file as a card in a card deck, and a 3D matrix file as the deck. Creating a 3D matrix file from a series of 2D matrix files is just a matter of concatenating the 2D files together. See Chapter 9 for examples of this.

### 3D Matrix to 2D Matrix

See Chapter 9 for examples of pulling 2D matrix files from a 3D matrix file.

## Adding Dimensions

A major theme throughout this book is that adding dimensions to your data can often help you analyze and visualize it better. By *adding dimensions*, we mean to consider more of your data as data *locations*.

For example, in Chapter 7 we showed how interpreting a dataset of color information as a 3-dimensional dataset can produce insightful graphs. In the same chapter, we showed how Jeanne Beeker's dataset could be visualized as a 6-dimensional scatter plot.

In Chapter 8, we returned to Dr. Beeker's dataset and visualized it as a 2-dimensional matrix. Here we used the *column and row indices* themselves as the data locations.

In Chapter 9, we visualized a series of 2-dimensional matrices and produced a single 3-dimensional matrix. The third dimension in this case was the *file number*. We also showed how we could split up that 3-dimensional matrix into a series of 2-dimensional matrices.

What's the point? It is important to play with the dimensionality (and the organization) of your data. By doing so you may discover knowledge hidden in your data that you never suspected. This can be illustrated by a final, somewhat more personal[*] example, described below.

## 1D Data to 2D Data: An Example

In this project we were doing 1-dimensional simulations of material falling spherically onto a star. These simulations produced several 1-dimensional datasets, such as 'density as a function of radius.' This was a time-dependent simulation, so we produced a new 1D dataset for every new time. Linegraphs of density vs. radius for several times are plotted below.

**Figure 11.44**
*Density as a function of Radius, for Several Times*

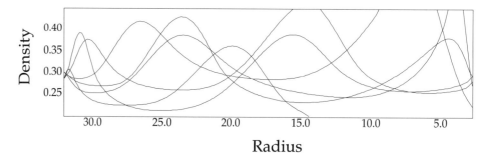

It was very difficult to analyze these 1-dimensional graphs and the relation of one time to another time. There was clearly something very regular going on, but it is difficult to isolate the regularity.

We decided to visualize the data as a single 2-D dataset rather than as a series of 1-D datasets. (The variable of *time* added the second dimension.) A grayscale plot of the resulting 2-D dataset is shown in Figure 11.45.

---

[*] Fortner, B., Lamb, F. K., and Miller, G. S. 1989, Nature, **342**, 775.

**Figure 11.45**
*Density as a Function
of Radius <u>and</u> Time*

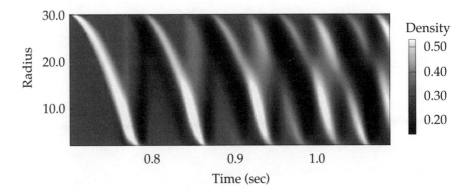

We were all surprised at the pattern we saw. The regularity of the simulation results was evident in ways that could never be seen in the linegraphs. (The white striations represent clumps of matter falling onto the stars.) The pattern gave us great insight into the simulation, and into the physical system that it describes.

Once again, the moral is to play with your data dimensionality. You may discover something interesting.

## Summary

This chapter was about converting data from one data organization to another data organization, and about changing data dimensionality. The most important conversion process is from column data to matrix data, and we described in detail how this is done. In particular, we showed how to *grid* column data, and then how to *fill missing data values*. The most complex fill missing data value routine is *kriging*, which we described in detail. We then discussed briefly how changing or adding dimensionality to your dataset can give you insight into your data.

# PART IV
# DATA FORMATS

In this book we have talked about how you can store your numbers (as ASCII Text, as integers, as floating point, etc), and how you can organize your numbers (as column data, as matrix data, etc). In this Part we discuss industry standard data formats that take care of some of these storage and organizational issues for you.

Chapter 12 briefly lists many of the formats in use for technical data. Chapter 13 goes into some detail on the HDF data format.

# CHAPTER 12
# DATA FORMATS

## Data Formats—Introduction

There are hundreds of data formats used by various disciplines for all sorts of data. In this chapter we talk about several of those formats. When evaluating whether to use a particular format, you should keep in mind the following questions.

### Questions to Keep in Mind

- Is the format *machine independent*? Can you write a file on one type of computer and read it on another type, without conversions?

- Is the format designed for storing *numerical data*, such as an array of numbers, or for storing *graphical data*, such as information on line drawings or images?

- Is the format *self describing*? In other words, can you read a datafile and extract all of its information without knowing anything about the datafile beforehand?

- How general is the format? Is the format specific to a particular type of data (geophysics, proteins, etc.), or can it store a variety of data types? Can it store different data organizations (matrix, column, polygonal)?

- Does the format support annotations inside the data? In other words, can you make notes about the data, and add labels to the data values and data locations, and store these inside the datafile?

- How widely available is the data format? Is it available as public domain software, as 'free with copyright,' or in a proprietary format? Is the format supported by any commercial vendors, or by a standards committee?

- How widely used and supported is the format? Is there a chance that your colleagues will be able to read your datafiles? Will *you* be able to read your datafiles ten years from now?

- Can you organize data within a single datafile? In other words, can you store multiple datasets in the same file, with some description of each dataset? Can you group datasets together inside the datafile?

- Does the format specify what the datafile looks like on the disk, or does it instead specify the way the file is written, through a subroutine library? *Disk-based* formats tend to be more portable between computers, and *subroutine library based* formats tend to have better programming support for reading and writing the files.

## A Selection of Data Formats

Below we describe several popular formats, answering some of the questions listed above. These descriptions are necessarily incomplete. If you have information on these formats, or on other formats not listed, please let us hear from you.

### BUFR

BUFR is a machine-independent data format standard for the World Meteorological Organization, used for self-defining meteorological and oceanographic data.

BUFR provides several decoders to convert integers and floating point data from an internal format to native formats. BUFR emphasizes the physical datafile format. The format is considered more machine independent than netCDF.

### CDF (Common Data Format)

CDF is a widely used data format standard developed by NASA for storing multi-dimensional gridded scientific data with user defined annotations. CDF is used in many disciplines and is supported by a wide variety of analysis and display applications.

CDF uses a column format to store the following number types: ASCII text, 16-bit and 32-bit integers, and 32-bit and 64-bit floating point numbers. A single dataset may be stored in separate files, which makes it easy to add data to an existing dataset.

CDF stores the data in XDR (external data representation) format, which is a nonproprietary standard for storing data to be machine-independent. XDR was originally developed by Sun Microsystems. XDR uses the IEEE standard for floating point numbers, and has been implemented for Suns, Vaxes, Macintoshes, IBMs, Crays, and other computers.

CDF is primarily a subroutine-library-based format. Because of this emphasis the subroutines are relatively simple to use. The dynamic addition of data to an existing CDF file is also a popular feature. In CDF the XDR implementation is machine-dependent, limiting the portability of the datafiles. The ability to annotate dimensions in CDF is weak.

## CGM (Computer Graphics Metafile)

CGM is widely used for computer graphics. Data for bit-mapped images and for vector objects, such as lines, circles, and polygons, can be stored in CGM files. A CGM *metafile* can be used to store  and organize several images in the same file. Individual images in the metafile can be accessed randomly.

CGM metafiles support the following number types: 8 bit, 16-bit, 24-bit and 32-bit integer, 32-bit and 64-bit floating point, and ASCII text data. CGM  files are considered fairly machine-independent.

CGM allows the incorporation of nongraphical and non-standardized information into the datafiles. Some people consider this extensibility a weakness, since some features added by a programmer may be unreadable by a CGM interpreter.

## DICOM (Digital Imaging and COmmunications in Medicine)

DICOM  is being developed by the American College of Radiology (ACR) and the National Electrical Manufacturers Association (NEMA) for the storage of medical image data. The standard is also known as ACR-NEMA, after the two sponsoring organizations.

DICOM image data is stored as a 2D matrix of unsigned or signed integers. Typically, the integers are 16-bits, although other bit depths are supported. The header for a DICOM file is a variable length record which describes the data. Support for 3D matrix data is being considered for the future. For more information contact David Snavely at NEMA (phone: 202/457-1965).

## DLIS  (Digital Log Interchange Standard)

DLIS, also known as RP66 (Recommended Practice 66), is a data format standard created by the American Petroleum Institute (API) for geophysical data. It is used to store  multi-dimensional arrays of various data types including floating point numbers, integers, and complex numbers.

DLIS is a self-describing data format which supports the use of annotations such as name, units, etc.. The specifications for RP66 are available from API (phone: 202/682-8375). Ask for document #811-09-306.

## DXF  (Data EXchange Format)

DXF is widely used in CAD (Computer Aided Design) applications to store polygonal data. Each data element in DXF consists of two lines. The first line consists of a 'type' code (indicating whether the data element an x-coordinate, a y-coordinate, etc.). The second line is the actual data (32-bit integer or floating point).

DXF was created for AutoCAD and was designed specifically for internal use by the company. However, the standard has since been adapted by many application software companies. For more information on DXF see the back of the AutoCAD manual.

## EPS  (Encapsulated PostScript)

Postscript is a proprietary graphics format developed by Adobe Systems, Inc. primarily for use in printers. It is actually a computer language for describing pages that consist of text, graphics, and raster images. When printing to a Postscript printer, your computer actually creates a Postscript computer program, and sends it to the computer inside the printer, which then executes the program. Postscript is primarily an ASCII standard, and is not designed for storing numerical data.

The EPS  (also known as EPSF) is a file format  for storing single page illustrations. The format uses a subset of the Postscript commands. Full Postscript files typically describe many pages graphically in the same file.

Most EPS files contain information on the size of the resulting illustration, a title, a list of fonts used by the illustration, and a machine-dependent preview version of the illustration (such as a PICT for Macintosh EPS files). This preview is used for on-screen display only, and is thrown away when printing.

## Erdas

Erdas is the standard format used by Erdas image processing software for remote sensing data usually from the global information satellites. The 2D matrix image data is stored as 4-bit, 8-bit, or 16-bit integers. Other analysis software packages, such as MultiSpec developed at Purdue University, use Erdas as their native format. More information is available from David Landgrebe at Purdue University (phone: 317/494-3486).

## FITS (Flexible Image Transport System)

FITS is used primarily by astronomers. It can store arrays of data with dimensions ranging from 1 to 999. The data types supported by FITS are: character, unsigned 8-bit integer, two's complement signed 16- and 32-bit integer, and IEEE single- and double-precision floating point numbers. FITS supports storing column data as ASCII text. Recently the FITS standard has been extended to storing binary column data (FITS BINTABLE format).

The original FITS standard was published in 1981 (Wells, *et. al.* Astron. Astrophys. Suppl. Ser. **44**, 363). FITS is the standard format for most major radio and optical astronomical observatories. It has been endorsed by NASA's Science Data Systems Standards Office and the International Astronomy Union.

FITS was originally designed to store images in a machine-independent format. It has since been extended to store numerical data. A FITS file contains a header and then the data. The header and the data may be stored in the same file or in separate files. The header is ASCII Text, whereas the data is usually binary.

Spyglass Transform reads FITS files directly.

## Flux

FLUX is an internal general data format for apE (animation production Environment), a visualization system developed at the Ohio Supercomputer Center.

## GRIB

GRIB was developed by the World Meteorological Organization for meteorological and oceanographic data. GRIB stores packed binary integer data in multi-dimensional arrays or in irregular grids.

## HDF (Hierarchical Data Format)

HDF is a scientific data file format developed at the National Center for Supercomputing Applications (NCSA) at the University of Illinois at Urbana-Champaign. It is a machine-independent binary file format standard for storing matrix, column, and polygonal data from a wide variety of disciplines. See Chapter 13 for more information on HDF. All Spyglass products read and write HDF files.

## IGES (Initial Graphics Exchange Specification)

IGES is a general format for transporting and storing polygonal data for CAD systems. It supports a more general set of geometry types than DXF and is designed to be system-independent.

## netCDF

netCDF is an extension of CDF developed by the National Center for Atmospheric Research (NCAR) and Unidata. netCDF stores multi-dimensional gridded data in a self-describing fashion and supports ASCII text, 16-bit and 32-bit integers, and 32-bit and 64-bit floating point numbers.

Each netCDF dataset contains information on dimensions, variables, and attributes. The dimension has both name and size and is used by all of the variables in the dataset. netCDF uses XDR for bytes, integers, and floating point numbers (see XDR writeup in CDR section above). Spyglass Dicer reads netCDF files directly.

## PDS (Planetary Data System)

PDS was developed by NASA's Jet Propulsion Lab (JPL ) to handle the data coming from various planetary exploration missions. PDS generally stores image data in 2D matrix form as 8-bit unsigned integers. PDS also supports column data, spectral data, and 3D matrix data. A PDS data file includes an ASCII text header describing the data; the header may be attached to or separate from the data. PDS is machine-independent and is intended to be a flexible formatting standard. The standard has evolved such that many implementations are now incompatible. For more information contact Marti at JPL (phone: 818/306-6017).

## PHIGS (Programmer's Hierarchical Interactive Graphics Standard)

PHIGS is a graphics standard that allows the user to specify geometrical objects and then refer to multiple copies of the object. An extension to this standard that allows shading and more complex geometries is called PHIGS+.

## PICT

PICT is the primary graphics standard for Macintosh computers. PICT can store image data as 1 bit, 2 bit, 4-bit, 8-bit, 16-bit, and 32-bit unsigned integers. Besides images, PICT files contain information on lines and characters. Because the use of PICT files is so widespread, many programs on computers other than the Macintosh will read or write PICT files. All Spyglass products on the Macintosh import and export PICT files.

## Plot3D

Plot3D is a visualization program which was developed at NASA Ames for use in computational fluid dynamics. It uses an internal data format of 3D matrix of binary data with either a uniform or a warped grid. Every dataset consists of two files: one with the grid description, and another with the data. The Plot3D file format is very specific for 3D computational fluid dynamics, which is both a strength and a weakness. For more information contact Pat Olsen at NASA Ames (phone: 415/604-4463).

## SEG-Y

SEG-Y was created by the  Society of Exploration Geophysicists (SEG)  for seismic data. The data is stored in multi-dimensional arrays of IBM-format floating point numbers. SEG-Y also supports 2-bit and 4-bit integer data although they are rarely used. SEG-Y is currently being revised. For more information contact SEG directly (John Bobbit at 713/267-5111).

## TIFF (Tagged Image File Format)

TIFF was developed by Microsoft and Aldus primarily to store images in a machine-independent way. Number types supported include: 8-bit unsigned integers, ASCII codes, 16- and 32-bit unsigned integers, and two 32-bit unsigned integers, where the first represents the numerator of a fraction and  the second represents the denominator.

TIFF data is stored one image at a time in a tagged data block. TIFF then defines a linked list of tag blocks. TIFF is one of the most commonly used standardized data formats, especially for the storage of image (2D matrix) data. For more information contact Aldus  (phone:  206/628- 2320)  or Microsoft (phone: 206/882-8080).

Spyglass Transform reads TIFF files directly. Spyglass Dicer can make use of TIFF files through a separate utility program.

# CHAPTER 13
# THE HDF STANDARD

## The Hierarchical Data Format (HDF)

HDF is an extensible, binary, public domain file format specification for storing data and images.[*] HDF files can store floating point data, scaling information, color images, text annotation, and other items. HDF originated at the National Center for Supercomputing Applications (NCSA) at the University of Illinois at Urbana-Champaign, where it was developed as a solution to the problem of sharing data among all of their different computers.

NCSA maintains and distributes a public domain software library to read and write the HDF format. It runs on a variety of computers including Macintosh, Sun, VAX, Silicon Graphics, and Cray UNICOS. The base code is written in C with both FORTRAN and C bindings supported for making calls to the HDF libraries.

Spyglass provides a Macintosh version of the libraries which are compiled with MPW C 3.1. A compiled library is provided so users of Language Systems FORTRAN and Absoft MacFortran II do not need a C compiler to read and write HDF files.

The HDF specifications and the HDF Library are in the public domain.

## Using HDF

With HDF it is easy to start with the easy-to-use calling interface and then move into the more powerful ones later. C and FORTRAN bindings help you read and write HDF files. For example, to write a FORTRAN character array which represents an 8-bit color image to an HDF file, the following HDF call is all that is required (for details see the HDF manual).

**Figure 13.1**
*HDF Call to Write
an 8-bit Image*

```
ret=DFR8putimage('myfile',image1,rows,cols,compressiontype)
```

Figure 13.2 is another example, this time of writing a 3-dimensional array of floating point numbers to a file.

---

[*] All Spyglass products use HDF as their primary data storage format.

**Figure 13.2**
*HDF Call to Write a 3D
Floating Point Array*

```
ret=DFSDputdata('myfile2',3,dimensions,data_array)
```

A single HDF file may contain several different types of objects. A fully rendered 24-bit image of a molecule may be stored in the same file as the data record containing the actual positions of the atoms in space. The file may also contain an ASCII text annotation notebook describing which molecule it is, etc.

## HDF Specifications

HDF is a data storage format developed for use with scientific visualization. It is growth-oriented, extensible, and hierarchical.

HDF is a binary format, random access file of bytes. The file is continuous, meaning that it is not broken up into blocks.

### HDF Header

Every HDF file contains a header. This header contains a directory of records inside the HDF file. An individual record could be an annotation, a matrix, an image—just about anything.

Every directory entry for a record contains a pointer to the record, the length of the record, and a 16-bit tag defining the type of record.

### HDF Tags

The tag values are allocated as follows:

- Tags 0-7999 are reserved for HDF core data types.
- Tags 8000-15999 are assigned by NCSA to anyone upon request/approval.
- Tags 16000-31999 are user available for development, etc.
- Tags 32000-65535 are reserved for HDF expansion.

### Core HDF Tags

The core HDF tags support the following types of records. Most of the record types listed below support data in any of the number formats listed in the next section.

- 8-bit color images
- 24-bit color images
- Color lookup tables
- 2D, 3D, and n-D matrix records
- Numeric scales for matrix records
- Annotations for matrix records (min/max, units, labels, etc.)
- ASCII text notebook for human-readable annotations
- Column data records
- Polygonal data records
- Record Groups: a group of records organized into a directory

## HDF Number Types

One tag type is used to specify the number type of the associated record. The number types that HDF supports are as follows.

- Two's complement integers, signed or unsigned, of any bit length
- Motorola, Intel or VAX byte ordering for integers
- Single-precision and double-precision floating point in IEEE, Intel, VAX, and Cray formats
- Signed and unsigned characters

## HDF Computer Types

Another tag type defines the type of computer on which the file was written. If the data is written into the HDF file in a machine-dependent format (as opposed to a standard format such as IEEE), then the reading computer can use this computer type code to translate the data.

- Category 1111    Sun, SGI Iris, Alliant, Macintosh, etc.
- Category 2221    VAX (VMS and Ultrix)
- Category 3331    Cray architecture (UNICOS, CTSS)
- Category 4441    Intel-based PC

# An Example HDF File

Figure 13.3 shows an HDF file that includes two images. Each image has three directory entries: an entry for the color lookup table (palette), an entry for the size of the image (dimensions), and an entry pointing to the actual data (raster image).

**Figure 13.3**
*Schematic of*
*Example HDF File*

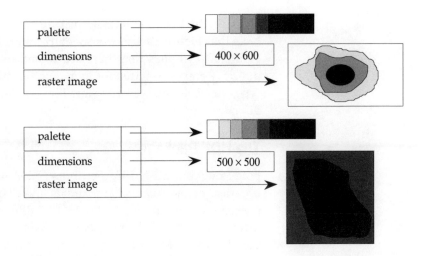

Listed below is the beginning of the HDF file Figure 13.3 represents.

**Figure 13.4**
*Listing of*
*Example HDF File*

| | Byte Number | Hex Value | Value | Item |
|---|---|---|---|---|
| *Header* | 1-4 | 0E 03 13 01h | ^N^C^S^A | Unique Number means HDF file(^N = control-N, etc.) |
| | 5-6 | 00 10 h | 16 | Number of Tags in Directory |
| | 7-10 | 00 00 00 00h | | Location of continuation directory (none here) |
| *Directory Entry 1* | 11-12 | 00 CAh | 202 | Tag type for 8-bit raster image |
| | 13-14 | 00 02h | 2 | Unique ID Number for this record |
| | 15-18 | 00 00 01 2Ch | 300 | Byte location in file for start of this record |
| | 19-22 | 00 03 A9 80h | 240 000 | Length of record (400×600) |
| *Directory Entry 2* | 23-24 | 00 C9h | 201 | Color Table (palette) |
| • | • | • | • | • |
| • | • | • | • | • |

Only the first of 16 entries in the directory is listed in Figure 13.4. Note that Figure 13.3 shows six entries in the directory, whereas Figure 13.4 implies that there are 16 entries. The additional directory entries are used for items such as number type, machine type, etc. The data records start immediately after the last directory entry.

## The HDF Package

Both Spyglass and NCSA distribute NCSA's public domain HDF libraries for the cost of the manuals and disks. Shipped with the package are two manuals, the HDF Calling Interfaces and Utilities manual, and the HDF Specifications manual. The source code is portable to the Macintosh, Sun Unix, VAX VMS, most other UNIX implementations, and Cray's UNICOS.

To contact Spyglass:

> Spyglass, Inc.
> P.O. Box 6388
> Champaign, IL 61826
> 217/355-6000

To contact NCSA:

> National Center for Supercomputing Applications
> University of Illinois at Urbana-Champaign
> 605 E. Springfield Ave.
> Champaign, IL 61820
> 217/244 -0072

# PART V
# BRINGING IT ALL TOGETHER

Now we return to the researchers and their projects that were introduced in Part I. In Part I we posed five questions about each researcher's numbers and data. In this part we summarize the answers to those questions.

# PART V
# BRINGING IT ALL TOGETHER

# Bringing it All Together—Introduction

Here we return to the five researchers introduced in Part I. We show how they analyzed and visualized their data, and refer to any problems they had along the way that were mentioned in the text. By studying the problems and solutions of these hypothetical people, you may develop new insights into your own data.

## Judy ReSyrch—Fan Simulation

**Judy ReSyrch** at the University of Dutch Harbor is researching the airflow through a desk fan, through the use of 3-dimensional computational fluid dynamical (CFD) simulations.

In Chapter 4 (Floating Point Numbers), we discussed the problems she was having when taking the difference of two numbers that were very close (The Riddle of the Stairstep Graph). To stop the difference of the numbers from being *digitized*, Dr. ReSyrch decided to use *double-precision floating point* numbers for all her data.

In Chapter 8 (2D Matrix Data), we saw that some of Judy's data was best stored as *2D matrix data*, not *column data*. Her simulation numbers were organized on a *uniform grid*. We also looked at ways she could visualize her 2D matrix data as *raster images, surface plots, contour plots,* or *vector plots*. A raster plot of one of her 2D matrix datasets is shown below.

*Figure V.1*
*Grayscale Plot of*
*ReSyrch Velocity Data*

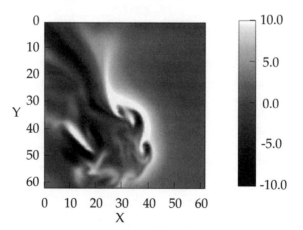

In Chapter 9 (3D Matrix Data), Judy was having difficulty visualizing her *3D matrix data*. We then looked at her data using the *slicing/dicing*, *isosurfaces*, and *transparency* 3D matrix visualization techniques. An example of an isosurface image with slicing/dicing of Judy's 3D dataset is shown below.

**Figure V.2**
*Isosurface with Two Slices and a Cutout of ReSyrch Velocity Data*

We can now answer the questions posed at the beginning of the book.

### How Are the Numbers Stored?

Dr. ReSyrch stores her data as *double-precision floating point* numbers.

### How Is the Data Organized?

Some of her data is stored as *2D matrix files*, while other datafiles are stored as *3D matrix files*.

### What Is the Dimensionality of the Data?

Judy's 2D matrix datasets nominally have two dimensions, and the 3D matrix datasets have three dimensions. However, her simulations are time-dependent, meaning that she has a series of datasets for different times. She could turn a series of 2D datasets into a 3D dataset, or a series of 3D datasets into a 4D dataset.

### Is the Data on a Grid?

Both Dr. ReSyrch's 2D matrix data and 3D matrix data are on uniform grids.

### What Is the Best Way to Analyze the Data?

Time-dependent CFD simulations can produce billions of numbers. By far the best way to analyze this deluge of data, at least initially, is with visualization. A single graphic, such as Figure V.2, can show millions of numbers in a second. The knowledge of which visualizations work best with different data comes with experience. CFD data is particularly well suited to raster image visualization, since the data tends to be on a uniform grid and is very rich in detail.

It may also be worthwhile to consider manipulating the data before visualizing it (looking at pressure *change* instead of pressure, for example), or modifying the dimensionality of the data. Either of these processes can sometimes produce fresh insights.

## Michael Astroe—FITS Data

**Mike Astroe**'s research is the Crab Nebula. He used an image from a compact disc of data from the Einstein X-ray satellite. In Chapter 2 (Bytes) Mike found that the data for his images was stored as *signed integers*, not as *unsigned integers*.

In Chapter 8 (2D Matrix Data) Dr. Astroe ran into a problem: most of the datapoints in his image were between 0 and 500, but some of the datapoints were very large (99999). These large values were actually coding for *missing data values*. When Mike ignored these missing data values, his data looked like the following.

*Figure V.3*
*Grayscale Image of Astroe*
*FITS File with Missing Data*

Mike used the *nearest neighbor* method described in Chapter 11 to interpolate those missing data values. The resulting image is shown below.[*]

---

[*] The images shown here are actually the logarithm of the original data, to compress the wide intensity range in the image. An inverse median filter was also run on the image to reduce the random noise still evident at the edges of the image.

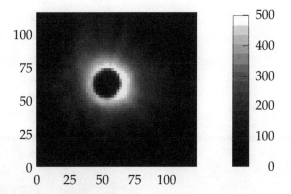

**Figure V.4**
*Astroe FITS Image with Missing Values Removed*

### How Are the Numbers Stored?

The original data was stored as a 16-bit signed integer FITS file. Mike's modified image was stored as floating point numbers.

### How Is the Data Organized?

The original data and the modified image were stored as 2D matrix files.

### What Is the Dimensionality of the Data?

The images all have two dimensions.

### Is the Data on a Grid?

As is true of most images, the data is on a *uniform grid*.

### What Is the Best Way to Analyze the Data?

Color raster imaging is a powerful visualization and analysis technique for images of all types. But beware: we modified the original data quite a bit to get the image shown in Figure V.4. When evaluating the importance of particular features in an image, it is vital that the data modifications are known and are taken into account.

## Dr. Tim Boans—MRI Scans

**Dr. Tim Boans** spent an afternoon taking a series of 2-dimensional MRI (Magnetic Resonance Imaging) images of the head.

In Chapter 3 (Integers), Dr. Boans was concerned that his images did not have enough detail. He then switched from storing the data as *8-bit bytes* to *16-bit integers*. Later in the same chapter, we

---

discussed Tim's problems with moving the data between computers: his scanner had a different *byte order* than his computer.

In Chapter 9 (3D Matrix Data), Dr. Boans took his *2D matrix* images and combined them into a single *3D matrix* dataset. A visualization of this dataset, using the visualization techniques of *slicing/dicing* and *isosurfaces*, is shown below.

*Figure V.5*
*Volumetric Rendering*
*of 3D Matrix MRI*

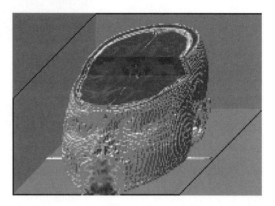

Later in the same chapter, we discussed how Tim could turn the 3D matrix dataset into a series of 2D matrix images, but in a different direction than the original data.

### How are the Numbers Stored?
Dr. Boans' data is stored as *16-bit unsigned integers*.

### How is the Data Organized?
The data was originally stored as a series of *2D matrix* files. These files were combined to form a single *3D matrix* file.

### What is the Dimensionality of the Data?
The data originally consisted of a series of 2-dimensional files. The resulting 3D matrix file had three dimensions.

### Is the Data on a Grid?
As is the case for most images, this data is on a *uniform grid*.

### What is the Best Way to Analyze the Data?
3D matrix visualization techniques are best for getting an overall feel for the datasets. Individual 2D matrix slices can show more

detail than 3D visualizations. Raster images using a grayscale color lookup table are popular for medical images.

## Jeanne Beeker—Solubility Experiments

**Jeanne Beeker** is studying the solubility of various compounds in certain solvents. She has tested 72 compounds with six solvents, looking for interesting correlations between the solubility of the compounds with the solvents used.

In Chapter 7 (Column Data), we showed how Jeanne's data could be analyzed either as a series of *six 1-dimensional* datasets (six solubility curves vs. compound number), or as a *single 6-dimensional* dataset (compound vs. solubility in the six solvents). We then showed how a 6-dimensional dataset could be visualized as a matrix of 2-dimensional *scatter plots*.

In Chapter 8 (2D Matrix Data), we showed how Dr. Beeker's data could even be visualized as a *2-dimensional* dataset (solubility vs. solvent number and compound number), shown below.

*Figure V.6*
*Solubility vs. Solvent Number and Compound Number*

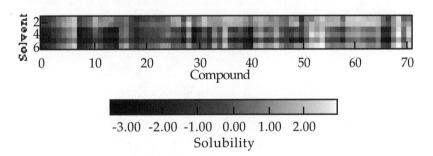

### How Are the Numbers Stored?
Dr. Beeker's data is stored as *ASCII text* numbers.

### How Is the Data Organized?
The data is stored as a *column* dataset.

### What Is the Dimensionality of the Data?
Take your pick. In this book we have shown how Jeanne's data can be considered *1-dimensional*, *2-dimensional*, or even *6-dimensional*. Other choices for data dimensionality are possible. This project

illustrates clearly that you should try many different choices for the greatest insight.

## Is the Data on a Grid?

When considering Dr. Beeker's data as a 6-dimensional dataset, we find that there is *no grid*. This means there is no regularity to the data locations (in this case, the solubility of the six solvents).

When considering her data as a 2-dimensional dataset, however, there is a *uniform grid*. Here the data locations are solvent number and compound number, which forms a 6 by 72 grid.

## What Is the Best Way to Analyze the Data?

Jeanne's project is perhaps the most conceptually difficult of our examples. She is looking for a pattern in the data, which in her case can probably best be done with statistical measurements of the data.

The visualizations of the data, such as the 6-dimensional scatter plot in Figure 7.19 or the grayscale image shown above, can help guide the statistical analysis by suggesting areas to examine more closely.

## Wolfram Herth—Ground Water Information

Wolfram Herth measured the groundwater level in a Texas county. He wants to visualize the data in a way that is clear to county commissioners and other policy makers. In addition, he needs to have the most accurate model of groundwater level that is possible, given the necessarily small number of measurements.

In Chapter 3 (Integers and Fixed-Point Numbers), Wolfram considered storing some data as *fixed-point numbers* to save disk space. He decided to use *ASCII Text* numbers for most of his data.

In Chapter 5 (ASCII Text Numbers), Mr. Herth ran into trouble storing his data as a *fixed format* ASCII text file. His linegraphics program did not know where one number ended and another one started. He corrected the problem by making sure that his numbers always had at least one space between them.

In Chapter 11 (Conversions), we showed how Wolfram's original dataset, shown as a grayscale image in Figure V.7, could be used to calculate a new 2D matrix dataset.

**Figure V.7**
*Grayscale Image of
Herth Dataset*

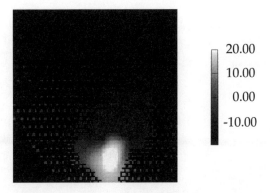

The best way to generate that 2D matrix dataset from Mr. Herth's data was through the use of *kriging*. An image of the results of the conversion is shown below.

**Figure V.8**
*Grayscale Image of Kriged
Herth Groundwater Dataset*

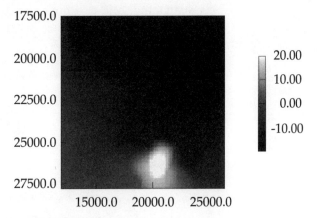

### How Are the Numbers Stored?
The original dataset was stored as a *fixed-format ASCII text* file. The interpolated 2D matrix file was stored as a *single-precision floating point HDF* file.

### How Is the Data Organized?
The original dataset was a column dataset. The interpolated file was stored as a 2D matrix file.

### What Is the Dimensionality of the Data?
Both the original and interpolated datasets had two dimensions.

### Is the Data on a Grid?

The original dataset had *no grid*, in that there was no regularity to the data locations. The interpolated dataset had a *uniform grid*.

### What Is the Best Way to Analyze the Data?

By creating the interpolated dataset, Wolfram can now use all of the powerful 2D matrix visualization techniques described in Chapter 8. In particular, the use of *surface plots* for this dataset would be particularly apt, since the data measures groundwater height.

## Summary

We hope the use of these five projects has helped to explain some of the details of technical data storage, organization, and visualization. We also hope that the examples will be useful as you think about the storage, organization, and visualization of your own data.

# GLOSSARY

**2D Matrix Datafile**   A datafile with two data locations and a single data value, where the data locations fit on a regular grid. See Chapter 8.

**2D Scatter Plot**  See *Scatter Plot*.

**3D Matrix Dataset**   A datafile with three data locations and a single data value, where the data locations fit on a regular grid. See Chapter 9.

## A

**ASCII Text Numbers**  ASCII text numbers are text strings, the same format used for conventional written material. Each ASCII text number uses a variable amount of space (one character or byte per decimal digit), has a variable range of values, a variable precision, and is human-readable.  See Chapter 5.

## B

**Bar Graph**  A way to graph 1-dimensional data. Each data value-data location pair is plotted as a vertical bar on an X-Y graph. See Chapter 7.

**Binary**  There are three types of binary numbers: *bytes*, *integers*, and *floating point numbers*. Every binary number is stored in a fixed amount of space with a fixed range of values and a fixed precision. The numbers are not 'human readable,' meaning that printing the file will produce garbage.  See Chapter 1.

**Bit**  Computers store everything as *bits*; each bit has a value of either 0 or 1. (*Bit* is a contraction for b̲inary digi̲t)  See Chapter 2.

**Byte**  Every normal computer deals with combinations of eight bits called a *byte*. The eight bits of a byte can represent 256, or $2^8$, distinct values.  See Chapter 2.

**Byte, unsigned**  See *Unsigned Bytes*

## C

**Cell-based**  A polygonal dataset where the data values are defined not at the data locations (as they are in a *node-based* dataset), but in *cells*. A cell is usually a polygon or closed surface defined by a series of data locations, also known as *nodes* or *vertices*.   See Chapter 10.

**Column Datafile**  A file where data is organized in the form of one or more columns placed side by side.  Typically ASCII text files with spaces or tabs between the column entries and line separators (CR, LF) between the rows.  See Chapter 7.

**Color Raster Imaging**   A way of visualizing data in a 2D matrix datafile as colors.  See Chapter 8.

**Color Table**   A lookup table that describes how data values map to colors.  Used in Color Raster Imaging.  See Chapter 8.

**Contour Plots**   A way of visualizing data in a 2D matrix datafile as a series of curves that connect equal values.  See Chapter 8.

**D**

**Data Description**   Items in a dataset that are the same for all values in the dataset.  See Chapter 6.

**Datafile**   A collection of data treated as a single item.  Often means a single disk file.  Synonymous with *dataset*.  See Chapter 6.

**Data Location**   In a dataset, the information needed to give a particular data value *organization* and *location*.  Synonym: *independent variable*.  See Chapter 6.

**Dataset**   Synonym for *datafile*.

**Data Value**   That information in a dataset which is your prime interest; synonym: *dependent variable*.  See Chapter 6.

**Denormalized Numbers**   See *Normalized Numbers*.

**Dependent Variable**   Analagous to *data value* in this book.

**Dimensionality**   The number of location values associated with every data value. Dimensionality of a dataset is not fixed; you can redefine elements of the dataset to manipulate the dimensionality. See Chapter 6.

**Double-Precision**   An 8-byte floating point number.  Double-precision numbers have much more precision than single-precision floating point numbers.  See Chapter 4.

**E**

**Extended Format**   An 80-bit floating point number.  More precision than double-precision floating point numbers.  See Chapter 4.

**F**

**Fixed Point Numbers**   In fixed-point arithmetic the position of the decimal <u>point</u> stays <u>fixed</u>. The equation is

$$y = m \times x$$

where $y$ is the actual stored value, $m$ is the multiplier, and $x$ is the original value.  See Chapter 3.

**Floating Point Numbers**   Binary numbers stored in computers using exponential notation. Each value is stored as two signed integers: one for the fractional part, and one for the exponent. This format is usually called single-precision floating point, or single-precision real. It is called floating point because the decimal <u>point</u> <u>float</u>s (moves) based on the value of the exponent. See Chapter 4.

## G

**Gridded Dataset** A two dimensional or three dimensional dataset with some regularity to the data locations. See Chapter 8.

## H

**HDF** Hierarchical Data Format, a flexible, standard, public-domain file format designed for sharing graphical and floating point data among different programs and machines. See Chapter 13.

**Header** In an ASCII text datafile, lines of text that precede the data and typically include a verbal description of the data. For binary files, the offset from the beginning of the file to the first data value. See Chapters 5 and 7.

**Hex** (Short for <u>hex</u>adecimal, or base 16) A compact representation of the binary representation of numbers. See Chapter 2.

## I

**Independent Variables** Analagous to *data location* in this book.

**INF** IEEE identifier that stands for infinity. A special floating point value that codes for infinity. See Chapter 4.

**Integer** A binary number that codes for integers (-1,23,0, etc). A 2-byte integer is called a *short integer* . An integer of 4 bytes or more is sometimes called a *long integer*. See Chapter 3.

**Isosurface** A 3D matrix visualization technique that connects data values of equal magnitude with a surface. See Chapter 9.

## K

**Kilobyte** $2^{10}$ bytes, or 1024 bytes, so 32K bytes is actually equal to 32 x 1024 or 32,768 bytes. See Chapter 2.

**Kriging** A sophisticated technique for filling in missing data values. See Chapter 11.

## L

**Linegraph** A way to graph 1-dimensional data. Each data value-data location pair is plotted on an X-Y graph. Symbols may or may not be placed at these points, then the points are connected by lines drawn in order of increasing X location. See Chapter 7.

**Long Integer** See *Integer*.

## M

**Megabyte** $2^{20}$ bytes, or 1,048,576 bytes. Therefore, 32 megabytes (32M bytes) equals 33,554,432 bytes.

**Missing Data Value** A location in a matrix datafile that does not have a data value. See Chapter 11.

## N

**NaN** IEEE identifier that stands for Not a Number. A special floating point value that codes for an invalid number. See Chapter 4.

**Nearest Neighbor Interpolation** Filling in missing data values using the nearest (by location) known data values. See Chapter 11.

**Node-based Dataset** A polygonal dataset in which the data values are defined at the data locations, also known as *nodes*. See Chapter 10.

**No-grid Dataset** A 2D or 3D matrix dataset with a uniform grid, where the grid values are not stored but assumed. See Chapter 8.

**Non-uniform Grid** A 2D matrix dataset where the spacing between the X and Y numerical scales is not uniform, but all numbers in a particular column have the same X value, and all numbers in a particular row have the same Y value. See Chapter 8.

**Normalized Numbers** A floating point number format that can store a larger maximum range of values than a denormalized number format with the same number of bits. See Chapter 4.

## O

**Octal** Octal digits (base 8) range from 0 to 7, and each octal digit represents three bits. An example of an octal number is 234o (o for octal). See Chapter 2.

**Offset** In fixed-point arithmetic, a constant added to the data value before storing it. See Chapter 3.

**Outlier** A data point that is higher or lower than the data region in which you are interested. The values are often removed using missing data routines. See Chapters 8 and 11.

## P

**Parametric Plot** A scatter plot with lines drawn between the plotted values. Parametric plots differ from linegraphs in that there can be multiple y values (data values) for every x value (data location). See Chapter 7.

**Polygonal Data** A column dataset that defines a set of polygons. See Chapter 10.

**Pseudocolor Imaging**   A synonym for *Color Raster Imaging*.

## R

**Range of Values**   The difference between the largest and smallest number which can be stored in a particular format.  See Chapters 2 through 5.

## S

**Scalar Datafile**   A matrix datafile where every data value represents a single number, as opposed to a vector.  See Chapters 8 and 9.

**Scatter Matrix**   A matrix of 2-dimensional scatter plots used to plot data of greater than three dimensions.  See Chapter 7.

**Scatter Plot**      Used for plotting a single 2-dimensional or 3-dimensional dataset. Both the X-axis and the Y-axis (and the Z-axis in the case of 3D data) correspond to the data locations. A representation of the data value is then plotted at that location.  See Chapter 7.

**Short Integer**   Usually means a 2-byte integer.  See Chapter 3.

**Signed Byte**   In signed bytes, one bit is used to represent the *sign*, and seven bits are used to represent the *value*. The initial (top) bit is set to 1 for all negative numbers. (This bit is often called the *sign bit*.)  See Chapter 2.

**Single-Precision**   A 4-byte floating-point number format.  See Chapter 4.

**Slicing/Dicing**   A 3D matrix visualization technique where individual 2D slices through the 3D volume are rendered as color raster images.  See Chapter 9.

**Sparse Matrix**   A 2D matrix with missing data values.  See Chapters 8 and 11.

**Streamlines**   Conceptual 'smoke bombs' used to help delineate paths in 3D vector fields. Each streamline is a line drawn in three dimensions tracing the path a particle would take through the data, if the data represented wind velocity.  See Chapter 9.

**Structured Grid**   In a structured grid, the information on nearest neighbors is implicit in the grid.  2D matrix datasets and 3D matrix datasets are examples of structured grids.  No-grids, Uniform-grids, Non-uniform grids, and Warped-grids are all examples of structured grids.  See Chapter 10.

**Surface Plots** In surface plots the data values of a 2D matrix are converted to a height of a rubber membrane above the plane and a perspective view is generated. See Chapter 8.

**U**

**Uniform Grid** A matrix datafile where the data locations are uniformly spaced in each dimension. See Chapter 8.

**Unsigned Bytes** Bytes with no sign bit, so all 8 bits are used to store data values. See Chapter 2.

**Unstructured Grid** In an unstructured grid, every data value contains information not only on its data locations, but also on its nearest neighbors. See Chapter 10.

**V**

**Vector Fields** Usually a 3D matrix file with a vector of three components defined at every data location. See Chapter 9.

**Vector Plots** Using vector arrows to map a 2D or 3D vector field. See Chapters 8 and 9.

**Volumetric Data** Data stored in a 3D matrix is often called volumetric because the numbers fill a volume. See Chapter 9.

**Volumetric Visualization** In volumetric visualization, each data value is converted to an intensity, then plotted. The resultant image, like a cloud, uses opacity and transparency as clues to data density. See Chapter 9.

**W**

**Warped Grid** (Also known as a *rubber sheet grid*) Every data value has an associated X,Y pair of data locations. Similar to unstructured grids, except the information on nearest neighbors is still implicit in the grid, as is the case in all structured grids. See Chapter 8.

**Weighting Functions** Curves that describe the influence of a known data value on a missing data value. See Chapter 11.

# INDEX

# 2

# 3

# 6

# 8

# A

# B

# C

# D

# E

# F

# I

# J

# K

# L

# M

# N

# O

# P

# R

# S

# W